CRANTOCK TALES

Written & Illustrated by

Ben Dobson

Crantock Tales

ISBN: 978-1-910181-79-9

Printed and Published in Great Britain by
BookPrintingOnline part or AnchorPrint Group Ltd 2020

Published: July 2020

Copyright © July 2020: Ben Dobson

All rights reserved. No part of this book may be reproduced or transmitted in any form or by other means without permission in writing from the author, except by a reviewer who wishes to quote brief passages in connection with a review written for insertion in a magazine, newspaper or broadcast.

Copyright permission was sought by the author for the use of the images used in this book, but where this was not possible and amendments are required, arrangements will be made at the earliest opportunity.

CONTENTS

Preface

Chapter   Page

1 Crantock and The Gannel 1

2 The Marchioness of Abercorn 21

3 Farmer William Johns 35

4 Master Mariner William Johns 51

5 Jane Johns – The Lady of Mystery 71

6 The Industrial Revolution 85

7 The Divided Society 107

8 Bohemian Crantock 121

9 Wreck and Rescue 139

10 Dr Edward Bouverie Pusey 165

PREFACE

This book began life as a series of short stories given to local audiences as part of Crantock Story Cafés between 2016 to 2020. The idea was to present a short story to encourage people to discuss and add to the information. The events were held in our pubs, cafés, community halls, church and chapel. As a result, each story led to further research that would inevitably lead to yet another story. The Cafés also stimulated local interest into the history of Crantock and the formation of an active heritage group in the village.

Each of the stories in this book has been researched through newspaper archives, county and parish records as well as sources such as Grace's Guide to British Industrial History, the National Archives, Project Canterbury and many more "Googled" and reliable references. In addition, the memories of local people and their research have been used as both catalysts and corroborators of the minutiae in the stories.

Ten stories have been chosen for this volume, dealing with a cross-section of people and events associated with Crantock, with especial focus on the nineteenth and early twentieth centuries. Crantock has a history that dates from the stone age and has seen many changes through the bronze and iron ages to possible Roman settlement, to the arrival of missionaries from Ireland and Wales and a founding church, to the establishment of a large collegiate church to rival Oxford and Cambridge, to sand storms that engulfed it, to the reformation, to a thriving harbour and farming community, to a transformation into a popular visitor attraction. All through these chapters in its life, one thing stands out, a continuous "sense of place", of a thriving community bound together by that special "Crantockness". I hope that that little book helps to intrigue and encourage the reader to share in these stories and to search for all the missing links and obvious errors!

CHAPTER 1

Crantock & The Gannel

In 1813, two men, William Daniel and Richard Ayton, set out on a voyage around Britain. William was an accomplished artist and it was his intention to produce a pictorial record of the entire coastline of Great Britain. He chose Richard, who was a trained solicitor from Manchester and also a writer and sailing enthusiast, as a companion with the intention of producing a series of illustrated books.

The journey was to take William over ten years as he only travelled during the summer months, spending the winter creating his illustrations. Unfortunately, the two men fell out after a couple of years, partly because of poor sales of their first set of books covering Cornwall, Devon and South Wales. The reasons for the lack of sales was partly because of the high production costs of the illustrations but also the highly political nature of the accompanying text provided by Richard. Richard was appalled by the poverty that they encountered over the first part of their journey and he was an enthusiastic supporter of social reform to address these issues. His writing reflected his opinions on the way in which the working classes were being treated by their employers; the very class of people at which the publication was aimed and the only people who could afford the price of the books. So, after two years they went their separate ways and William continued alone around the rest of the country, finally returning to Cornwall in 1823. It is generally considered that the later books, illustrated and written by William, lacked the detailed accounts of life amongst the working classes around the coast that Richard had described in such rich detail.

Richard Ayton's description of their approach into the Gannel is a good example of his realism: "*This creek was formerly more considerable than it is at present, but has received a more than common share of mischief that pervades every haven on the Cornish coast, and is so blocked up by the sand forced into it by storm from the north and west, that it cannot admit vessels of more than thirty tons. Near the mouth of the Ganal there is a little*

village, called Carantoc, which, like other places inhabited only by the poor, is mean and dirty. Here was anciently a large town, a collegiate church, dedicated to St Carantocus, a disciple of St Patrick; and here too, where now little meets the eye but the cheerless desert of sand, once stood a college, which could boast of as high antiquity, if not as high repute, as any college in Oxford. There is something exceedingly mournful in the contemplation of scenes of desolation, which learning and religion once combined to render illustrious, where once flourished colleges and cathedrals, now mouldered into dust. At Carantoc, once peopled by students and professors, once the seat of holy eloquence and meditation, there is now one deep silence, or nothing heard but the roaring of the sea and the howling wind. As its honours live only in history, we did not pause long to examine its sands, but sailed again down the Ganal, at present an inglorious stream, though formerly, perhaps, (so fancy may plead) as well known to the muses as the Isis and the Cam."

A sad description of both the river and Crantock but yet there were brighter days ahead as the river was revitalised by the mining activities of Newlyn Downs and Perranporth over the next fifty years. Indeed, there must have been commercial shipping in the river at the start of the nineteenth century as both the lead and zinc mines of Newlyn and the iron mines from Perranporth were already active.

Crantock has always been inextricably linked to the river Gannel. In medieval times, the river would have been very different from what we see today. Much of the river was silted up during the working of the mines on Newlyn Downs during the period from the early eighteenth until the end of the nineteenth century. Before this, in all probability, the river would have been navigable well up towards Newlyn East, certainly to Gwills and perhaps even as far as Trewerry. The manor at Trerice was almost certainly accessible from the river when it was first built in the fifteenth/sixteenth centuries. The Admiralty had an interest in the river, and was responsible for some of the dredging in the nineteenth century. It is an established understanding that the river was a recognised haven of shelter and marked as such on Admiralty charts (although not confirmed).

The river represented the Western limit of the port of Padstow, Port Gaverne being the Eastern boundary. Sea-borne trade within this port region would not be liable to harbour dues and thus it is entirely likely that the river was used as a trading post for slate being carried to the south and west of Cornwall. It is understood that Penpol was at one time referred to as Truro quay where slate was landed and loaded onto wagons for transport to Truro during the rapid expansion of the city in the eighteenth century. There is still some evidence of the route of the cart-track running through Rejerrah and across to Zelah via Scotland road.

One important man-made feature that maintained navigability of the river was the training wall, locally referred to as the breakwater, that ran from Point Noe (the point of no return) seaward towards Salt cove. It is not known when this structure was first installed, but its original construction, lost to view in the 1980's when it was rebuilt with granite boulders, consisted of large vertically mounted slabs of slate, much like a large version of the stone hedges to be seen on the local headlands. A similar form of construction can be found at Port Isaac in the remains of the quay that has been dated to Elizabethan times. Certainly, the river would have been much different before any silting and, from the current landscape, it is not too difficult to imagine a broad estuary stretching much further inland than Trevemper. This would have contained a huge volume of water at high-tide, all of which would have drained back to sea as the tide ebbed. This "sluicing", coupled with the training wall, would have maintained a deep and navigable channel well inland from the current river mouth. Further, the lower river bed would have led to far swifter incoming tides than seen today. This is highlighted in some of the accounts of people and animals being overwhelmed by fast in-rushing tides and associated whirlpools and eddies during the nineteenth century.

The history of the training wall is not documented and maps of the area offer little assistance as the structure has never been marked, even on the most recent Ordnance Survey maps. Its presence can only be assumed from the course of the river shown on any maps.

The earliest map of the area is a sketch drawn by the Board of Ordnance in 1808 as part of a wide coastal survey in preparation for a potential invasion by the French. The 1808 sketch clearly shows the river aligned along East Pentire, suggesting that the training wall was operational at the time. This map also shows a substantial river running inland as far as Trevemper, above which the river valley is much as it is today. This is not surprising as lead and zinc mining had been conducted on Newlyn Downs since the mid-eighteenth century when the first Newcomen steam engines were installed to drain the mines. The drained water, and associated slurry, was discharged directly into the river.

The first definitive map of Crantock was drawn in 1839/40 to support the Tithe Apportionment Register of the area. This map was surveyed by Alexander Withers, a sixty-three year old who lived in St Agnes. He was employed as a Land Surveyor and would have spent most of his life supporting the mining industry with maps. In 1838, a map drawn by Withers was used as evidence in a dispute at St Agnes over the ownership of the mineral rights, valued at over £60,000, associated with an area of land known as the Bolenna estate. John Williams, of Scorrier House and Thomas Trelease believed that the rights had been included in a sale agreement with Charles Carpenter. The area, including the Bolenna estate, had been mapped in 1822 by Withers, under instruction from Mr Williams. The trial lasted for four days and was considered, at the time, to be unprecedented in establishing the mining rights of landowners. The reports of the trial ran over many pages in the local papers and eventually resulted in the jury dismissing the claims of Williams and Trelease and finding in favour of Carpenter.

Withers' map of Crantock is extremely accurate and can be super-imposed almost exactly over the "Google maps" image of the area. It clearly shows that the river was constrained against East Pentire. It also shows that the beach was much as it is today (2020) after all of the sand dune erosion. There are cliffs running across the beach above the high-watermark on the West Pentire side with a field where today there is scrub and dune. On the Gannel side, there are exposed cliffs from the present day surf-life saving club hut around to the Fernpit. A comparison between the 1808 sketch and the map of Withers confirms that the cliff-line that has now emerged was also evident at the beginning of the nineteenth century. The major difference between these two maps is the presence of enclosures on Rushy Green on the north side of the Green lane path in 1840 compared with open sand-dunes in 1808.

There are also Ordnance Survey maps from the early nineteenth century that show the river running against East Pentire. However, the Ordnance Survey map of 1880 clearly shows that the river had moved to a new course that runs across the beach from Point Noe. Subsequent maps show the river alternating between the constrained course against East Pentire and running across the beach. It is possible that some remedial work may have been carried out to the wall by the Admiralty around the time of the First World War, perhaps to provide a potential haven for shipping. In addition, as described in newspaper accounts of accidents on the beach, the river appears to have changed its course at various times; sometimes against East Pentire and sometimes meandering across the beach.

Crantock is old, as evidenced by the discovery of pottery from the bronze age Beaker people during the construction of a new housing development in 2019. In fact, Crantock is surrounded by evidence of bronze and iron age settlements from between 3000BC to 2000BC. There is also evidence to indicate that the area was inhabited from a much earlier stone age. One of the most well defined bronze age settlements is the enclosure on the end of the Kelsey's opposite Chick island. There are many more bronze and iron age remains scattered around the parish that indicate an permanent population living in the area.

The church of St Carantoc was founded around the fifth century, based on an early Christian settlement, Langorroc (also Langurroc) ("Lann" meaning an enclosure). There are suggestions that the lay-out of the village is reminiscent of early Roman settlements, with the church in one rectangular plot, an unusual form amongst Cornish churches, and the main village in an adjoining rectangular compound. Whilst there is little concrete evidence to support this theory, the fact that the river provided reasonably safe access along a significant stretch of coastline, makes it likely that the sea-going Romans could have established an outpost in the area. This idea is supported by evidence of a Roman presence at Tintagel, that has been dated to around the 3rd or 4th centuries.

St Carantoc is reputed to have been born in Ceredigion, West Wales. He is believed to have travelled through Ireland (County Meath), Cornwall and Brittany (Carentec) and has tenuous links with King Arthur. Numerous skeletons were discovered in 1856 to the north and west of the church, when they were digging house foundations, probably St Ambros, that date to medieval times.

The site of the existing church pre-dates the Norman conquest and it is described in the Doomsday Book (1086), by which time it is a collegiate church with a number of canons. There were a number of collegiate churches in Cornwall, perhaps the most well-known being Glasney at Penryn. The collegiate churches were monastic foundations administered by canons who were priests but who had not taken holy vows and were thus able to own land and mix with the local community. The church would have been the focal point for the village, owning most of the surrounding land and employing many of the local inhabitants.

By 1291, the collegiate college was a significant establishment with ten canons which would have made it of comparable size to the collegiate college at Glasney, as well as Oxford and Cambridge. Indeed, there are indications that there were connections between Crantock and Oxford that continued through the life of the college. The church is the only building associated with the original college that survives today. In 1377

Bishop Brantyngham ordered the Deans and Canons to take action to save the central tower. When the Bishop died in 1394 he left £40 to the church to undertake the necessary repairs. However, the funding came too late and the central tower collapsed in 1412 and was not replaced.

In addition to the church building, there were smaller chapels, such as one dedicated to St Ambrusco, within the confines of the village. Most likely there were other small chapels scattered around, certainly there is evidence of another to the north of the church. The church and associated college continued to be an important institution until the late fifteenth/early sixteenth century. However, a visitor, John Leland remarked in 1536 that there were only four canons left and many of the college buildings were in a state of disrepair and sand was beginning to engulf the grounds. The college was finally dissolved by Henry VIII around 1548 and all of the grounds were confiscated and handed over to the Cole family based at Trerice manor.

One of the most famous students at the college was John Tregonwell (Tregunnel?) who went on to Oxford, where he obtained his doctorate. He served as proctor to Henry VIII and was a key figure in the annulment of his marriage to Catherine of Aragon in 1533. Tregonwell was Principal Judge of the Lord of the Admiralty. He was also the principal agent for the king and Thomas Cromwell in the dissolution of the monasteries before eventually moving to Middleton in Dorset. He was knighted in 1553 for his services to the king and, despite his involvement with the dissolution of the monasteries, he served Queen Mary (Bloody Mary), who mounted an aggressive campaign to re-establish Catholicism when she assumed the throne.

After the dissolution of the college, the buildings were both over-run with sand and probably dismantled to provide building materials for the village. It appears that there were several major storms during the sixteenth century that caused considerable damage and sand inundation along the north Cornish coast. Settlements at Gwithian, Perranzabuloe and Crantock were overwhelmed by sand, perhaps aided by excessive harvesting of the native maram grasses that would have been used to thatch many of the buildings.

The church continued to serve as the parish church for Crantock and during the nineteenth century is was very much at the centre of activities with regular vestry meetings. Vestry committees evolved through the seventeenth and eighteenth centuries as a means of managing both the parochial and secular affairs of communities. During the nineteenth century, Crantock church provided the meeting place for the Vestry committee. One of the principal secular actions of the committee in the early nineteenth century was the overseeing of the Poor houses in the village. The whole country suffered major unemployment after the Napoleonic wars and Cornwall was no exception, although the booming mining industry provided significant opportunities. In 1834, because Vestry committees were being overwhelmed by the magnitude of the unemployment, responsibility for managing the Poor houses was transferred to elected guardians. Later, in 1850, the Vestry's Act finally separated parochial and secular functions and the latter became the forerunners of today's parish councils.

In 1867/8, a new parsonage was built on West Pentire road in part of Gustory Meadow, a piece of land owned by the Johns family (Thomas and Edward Lawer Martyn Johns) that they sold to the Church commissioners for £175. An adjoining Parish Room was added in 1895.

Unfortunately, by the end of the nineteenth century, Crantock church had become extremely dilapidated and was being used partly as a builder's store. A contributing reason for the decline of the church was the rise of Methodism across Cornwall. A Methodist chapel was built in the village in 1872 at which the famous Cornish preacher Billy Bray is said to have delivered services.

The church fortunes were reversed by the arrival of a new vicar, Father George Metford Parsons in 1894. Parsons, a "high-church" (anglo-catholic priest) arrived from the Church of the Holy Nativity at Knowle, Bristol. Over the next eight years he completely refurbished the church, vicarage, church barn and cattle house. He engaged the Plymouth based, but Cornish born, architect Edmund Sedding to undertake the restoration, with a Mr Nicholls as the principal builder supported by local craftsmen. Parsons managed the design and manufacture of a completely new set of stained-glass windows that are amongst the finest in the Country. The detailed design was undertaken by Charles Tute who was based in Gray's Inn, where the windows were also manufactured. Michael Swift has written a comprehensive and interesting description of the stained-glass at Crantock.

A new screen was designed and installed by another Plymouth based company Rashleigh Pinwill & Co. This company is interesting because it was based on three sisters (there were seven in total); Mary Rashleigh, Ethel and Violet Pinwill who were the daughters of the Reverend Edmund Pinwill and his wife Elizabeth. Edmund was appointed vicar of Ermington church in Devon in the late 1800's. He was determined that his daughters should have a profession so he set them to work alongside a team of craftsmen restorers who came to Ermington in 1884. One of their first large commissions was the pulpit at Ermington that they completed in 1889.

By 1900, the sisters had moved to Plymouth where they shared business accommodation with the architect Edmund Sedding, who had also been responsible for the restoration of Ermington church. It was through his patronage that they received many of their orders. It was extremely unusual for this period to have a business run by women, in fact their company name, Rashleigh Pinwill, appears to have been deliberately chosen to give the impression that it was run by a man. Over the next few years both Mary, who had been the initial driving force, and Ethel left the company so that by 1909, Violet was the sole owner. Violet continued to run the business, with moves to larger premises and the use of more automated tooling rather than individual wood carvers, until the 1950's. She died in 1957 by which time examples of the Pinwill woodwork could be found in over 300 ecclesiastical buildings in Cornwall and Devon.

Parsons was clearly very enthusiastic and a successful fund raiser to complete the task of renovating what had become an extremely dilapidated set of buildings. In 1900 he wrote an appeal in the Royal Cornwall Gazette, noting that he had raised close to £3000, although only about £430 had come from the parishioners. A single donor had funded the new screen and stalls. Parsons remarked that none of the tithe rents raised in the parish were provided to the clergy as was their original intent! He calculated that the average (legal) earnings for a Crantock inhabitant was only £25 so he was appealing to the wider community to help to save what he considered to be a unique ecclesiastical relic.

The church was reopened by the Bishop of Truro in July 1902 and was accompanied by a comprehensive description of the church in the Royal Cornwall Gazette. It was remarked that *"Cornish architecture stands almost on the lowest rung in the scale of English art"*! The restoration fund had reached over £4000 with additional, individual, family donations provided to cover the costs of the new stained-glass windows. It was noted that the Duchy only provided around 10% of the necessary funding. The final addition was a new clock, built by Lord Grimthrope the designer of Big Ben, that was installed in 1904.

After completing the restoration, the church regained some of its previous worshipers, although Metford Parson's strict adherence to the Anglo-Catholic principles was not entirely welcomed in the village. In 1905 he closed the church to visitors because women were not covering their heads when they entered. His actions made the National press!

George Metford Parsons remained at Crantock until his death in 1924. He was predeceased in 1921 by the architect Edmund Sedding who is buried in the churchyard.

The church, in its long-life, has overseen a village and river that have changed considerably since its foundation. The village was very much focussed on agriculture, fishing and, in the early years, the business of the church college which would have been the major employer in the region until the reformation. Whilst records probably exist in the archives of the bishop of Exeter, there are local anecdotes that are likely remnants of stories handed down through generations.

In the beginning of the 18th Century, Crantock was divided between a small number of landowners based on the surrounding manors that included: Treago, Cargoll, Rialton, Tregunnel and Trerice. The church had been the major landowner up until the reformation (1548), when the land was confiscated and the majority given to the Cole family from Trerice Manor. It then passed through numerous owners (Lewis, Goldingham, Lutterell) and became more fragmented. A significant proportion of the "church-lands" seems to have ended in the ownership of the Johns family by the late 18th Century.

In 1798, under an act of Parliament, an assessment was made of the Proprietors (Landowners) and occupiers of the land in Crantock for the purposes of calculating a Land Tax. Surprisingly, the Bishop of Exeter is cited as a significant owner of land at Trevemper and to the East of the parish. Lord Falmouth also figures with interests in Pentire and throughout the centre of the village (Churchtown). There are a number of absentee landlords; Sir Francis Wynn (who owned several parcels identified as Lutterals – church grounds?), Sir William Lemon (of the Truro Lemon family), Lord Arundell (who ran up huge debts so that much of his land was sold off in 1808) and Lord Galloway - mainly Pentire properties. A number of "local" yeomen are also listed as landowners, including William Martyn, William Tinney, William Johns, John Johns, Mr Gavid and Mr Blewitt.

From the beginning of the nineteenth century, the history of Crantock can be tracked through newspaper archives. This period has seen the transition from a community firmly based in agriculture and the sea through a brief period of industrialisation to the current reliance on tourism. This book is primarily focussed on the nineteenth century during which the old feudal system of society diminished under the impact of the industrial revolution. Property-ownership became a reality for a much wider section of society and regional, national and international migration became possible. Crantock has a very long history stretching back thousands of years, much of which has been because of the river Gannel and the access it provides along a particularly hazardous section of coast. It has always been attractive to visitors, even in the nineteenth century there were holiday homes and during the early twentieth century professional people and artists from all disciplines could be found enjoying the village.

Despite all the changes, Crantock remains very much "community based", probably because its core is focussed in the small valley that runs down to the river that has always been a central feature. It has also managed to retain traditional village amenities including a shop, pubs, church/chapel and village hall, partly because the proportion of second and holiday homes has not become excessive. In addition, the village continues to create community based events such as the Bale-Push, village show and music concerts. Whether this "sense of place" will survive the expansion on the periphery and the continued growth of Newquay will be interesting to watch.

CHAPTER 2

The Marchioness of Abercorn

The Marchioness of Abercorn, was the largest ship to be driven ashore on Crantock beach and it provides both a glimpse into life in Cornwall in the mid-nineteenth century and an introduction to the Johns family and one of the most intriguing Crantock tales; that of Jane Trinidade.

The story takes place in 1847, when Queen Victoria had been on the throne for nearly 30 years. The Irish potato famine was at its height and, in fact, it had crossed into the South West where it had devastated the crop at the same time as there had been two very poor grain harvests. In the summer of 1847, grain prices were so high that the cost of bread was becoming beyond the reach of many. In the summer, there was deep unrest in Cornwall that led to the St Austell bread riots. Tin miners and china clay workers, believed that grain was being shipped out of Cornwall because the merchants could get a better price up-country and overseas. Fortunately, the summer of 1847 saw the best harvest for years and grain prices slumped to their lowest levels ever and the unrest subsided.

The Marchioness of Abercorn ran ashore during a violent storm at 9am on Wednesday, 8 December 1847. She was an 875 ton, three masted barque carrying a cargo of 1,300 tons of timber bound for London. She had a crew of twenty nine on board including the skipper, Captain James Docherty (there are various spellings of his name; Dogherty, Hegarty etc.) and she had sailed from Cork a few days earlier. The ship was named after Lady Abercorn, a daughter of the Duke of Bedford who was married to James Hamilton, Marquess of Abercorn and Lord Lieutenant of Ireland. Lady Abercorn was born in 1812 and died, at the ripe old age of 92 in 1905. She left thirteen children (only one of her children died before reaching maturity), all of whom married into prominent English aristocratic families. Alec Douglas-Home, Prime Minister, was one of her great-great grandchildren and Princess Diana and Sarah Ferguson were also amongst her descendants.

The Marchioness of Abercorn's voyage to London, with a cargo of timber, had started, as many of her voyages had done in the past, from Quebec. In fact, she had been built in Quebec ten years before the accident by Allan Gilmour and Co. The Gilmour family originated from Glasgow and had started trading in lumber with Canada in the 1820's. Several of the family had worked and lived in Canada although they all appear to have returned to Scotland when they grew old. Canada had become a key source of timber for the UK during the war with France when the Baltic ports were blockaded. Together with three other Scottish families, the Rankins, Pollocks and Ritchies, the Gilmours had become very successful timber importers. This was because of the way in which they managed to corner much of the Canadian market by pre-emptively buying the timber in rafts as it was being floated down the St Lawrence river to Quebec.

As the timber trade boomed with the increasing demands in UK, driven by the industrial revolution, the Gilmour's realised that shipbuilding would also be a profitable business and they developed a number of ship building yards in the Quebec area. By the mid-1800's the Gilmour's were probably the largest ship builders/owners in the world. At this time, they divided their business interests; the timber trade being run from Liverpool and shipping trade from Glasgow.

At 875 tons, the Marchioness of Abercorn was one of the Gilmour's largest vessels, a three masted barque of around 140ft long that was registered through their Glasgow offices with Lloyd's Register of Shipping. Lloyd's Register began life in 1760 as the Society for the Registry of Shipping based at the London coffee shop of Edward Lloyd. The aim of the Society was to provide merchants and insurance underwriters with detailed records of the condition of a ship based on surveying against a formal set of standards. The Register Book detailed the conditions of hull and equipment as well as recording the type of vessel, builders, owners, materials and age.

By the time that she met her fate on Crantock beach it seems that the Marchioness had been sold on to new Owners, John Power(?), Thomas Parkman, A Thompson and G Roberts. Captain Docherty appears to have been appointed as captain soon after the Marchioness entered service and remained with her when she changed ownership. Captain Docherty was probably from Limerick.

During the mid-1800s, there were many ships engaged in the Irish (and Cornish) emigration to Canada and the import of timber. The Cornish emigration was driven by a significant down-turn in the mining industry as cheaper, overseas sources were being developed.

The Marchioness became a regular trans-Atlantic trader, carrying emigrating passengers from the UK to both Canada and US and returning with cargoes of timber and, in winter, sugar cane from the southern US ports.

In the 1846/47 she was one of the principal transport ships for Irish emigrants who were escaping from the potato famine. During this period, she would carry up to 500 passengers from the Irish ports of Cork and Londonderry to Quebec and, in the winter, when the St Lawrence would freeze, New Orleans. She was able to complete the round-trip in about 44 days (25 out and 19 return). The Irish emigrant ships became known as the Famine or Coffin ships and some of them were infamous for the overcrowding of passengers that they would carry and the extreme conditions on-board. It was a lucrative business and many old and decrepit ships were pressed into action to exploit this emigration. In April, the brig

Exmouth was wrecked on Islay with 250 emigrants bound from Derry to Quebec. Only 3 survived. By June there were over 40 ships moored over 2 miles along the St Lawrence with 14,000 immigrants waiting to enter through the Grosse Island immigration centre that only had 150 beds and very limited accommodation. In 1847, over 100,000 Irish immigrants had entered Canada and North America. It is estimated that over 20% (1 in 5) died from typhoid either on passage or after arrival. Conditions were horrendous. In fact, it seems that conditions were far worse on these migration ships than on the slave traders. This was because slave ship owners only got paid when they got to their destinations. Thus, they carried doctors on board to treat the slaves. Migrants "paid up front" and so there was little incentive to provide medical cover during the trip. Typhoid could kill many during the voyage (in one instant over 140 died from a total of 400) and those that reached Canada were often herded into poor accommodation where the disease claimed yet more lives.

From the Grosse Island records, the Marchioness had completed an "outward" voyage prior to her fateful trip and had landed over 400 immigrants (including 6 dead) from Londonderry at the Quarantine Station on 1 August.

Her return voyage that was to end on Crantock beach was quite eventful. After a storm in mid-Atlantic, she was badly damaged and had to divert into Cork to effect repairs to her masts and rigging. Whilst in Cork she embarked a fresh crew of 29 under the Master.

The Marchioness left Cork, bound for London, but soon after leaving, she ran into yet another storm in the Bristol Channel. The ship again got into difficulties and was driven down the north coast of Devon and Cornwall. She ended up, damaged and heading across Newquay bay. It seems that the crew may have confused Trevose light (that had only been commissioned six days before on 1 December) with that of Lundy so that they thought they were heading towards the relative safety of Padstow. Whatever the cause, she ended up being swept past Newquay's Towan Head with her sails torn and one of her masts broken and hanging in the rigging. A pilot gig managed to get close to the ship off the headland, but the ebb tide and heavy seas prevented any rescue and she eventually ran ashore on the west side of Crantock beach.

It was around 9 o'clock in the morning and close to low water when she drove ashore with the seas breaking over her. She appears to have lost all but one of her boats and everything else on deck. She also had nine feet of water in her hold. A coast-guard crew, mustered after she ran past Newquay, under Mr Llewellyn, succeeded in firing lines over the ship using their Dennett's rocket system, but the ships' crew was unable to secure any of them.

Four of the crew succeeded in launching the last of their remaining boats but it was overwhelmed and, whilst two managed to scramble back to the ship, the other two were drowned. However, a boat was launched from the beach by William Johns, William Found and William Darke and succeeded in bringing four of the crew ashore and attached hawsers between the ship and the shore. The fact that they were able to launch a boat at low tide suggests that it came from Vugga Cove that probably accommodated a number of small boats. It could also act as a refuge for small coastal ships bound for the Gannel during rough weather. A third man was drowned trying to come ashore using one of the hawsers. The sad thing is that the remaining crew were all recovered alive later in the day as the ship was driven further on-shore. The general view was that the ship would soon break up and it was considered a total wreck.

An inquest was held on Monday, 13 December before the Coroner, J Carlyon, into the deaths of the three crew members. The body of Joseph Penn, was recovered near Vugga Cove on Saturday 11 December and that of James Cotter, who had tried to escape in the ships' boat, was found at Salt cove on the Monday morning. The body of the third man, James Prim (or it may have been Owen O'Harren, there are varying descriptions of the names), had not been recovered. In fact, his body did not come ashore until the end of February. A verdict of "Accidentally drowned" was recorded. The first two seamen, Penn & Cotter are buried in Crantock churchyard (and the church records confirm this), although their grave-markers have now disappeared.

The remainder of the ships' company were well cared for and letters were sent to both the Royal Cornwall Gazette and West Briton thanking local people for their help. In particular, the Master thanked Stephen Burridge (Collector of Customs), Capt. Nott (Inspecting Commander of Coast Guard), R B Hellyer (Agent for Lloyd's, with whom the cargo was insured) and Richard Stephens of Pentire House.

The ship owners specifically thanked Henry Croker (aged 37) who was a carpenter and also ran the Ship inn in the centre of Crantock village.

By the 17 Dec the ship was still intact and resting with her bows facing offshore but none of the cargo had yet been saved. However, the ships' crew had been transported to Hayle where they embarked on the Cornwall steamer for Bristol on Tuesday 14 December. The Hayle steamer Brilliant (that sailed once a week from Hayle to Bristol via St Ives and Ilfracombe) had just had new boilers fitted and this was probably her first voyage after the refit. It would cost 2 guineas to transport the family wagon, 25s for the horse and 16s for a saloon cabin! Four years earlier, the Brilliant had towed the carcass of a large whale into the Gannel while on passage to St Ives.

The cook (*"a very intelligent black"*), gave an account of the storm that had driven their ship ashore. It appeared that they had set sail from Cork on Sunday, 5 December, with the wind from the West-North-West. However, on the Monday they ran into high winds and their sails were split and some of their spars carried away. The crew had all embarked in Cork under terms of £3/man for the run to London.

Eventually the timber cargo was off-loaded under the supervision of Lloyd's and probably stored in what is now the Beach Road car-park in preparation for sale. But on Wednesday, 1 March, Richard George was apprehended in the act of carrying away a deal plank from the stored timber. An accomplice managed to escape. According to the 1841 census, Richard George was the publican of the Miner's Arms, now Wayside, Halwyn. The local magistrate (Reverend Edward) committed George to the local assizes where his case was heard before the end of the month. He was charged with the theft of the plank (property of Bernard Hall & Co, Liverpool). The cargo had been in the charge of T R Avery of Boscastle, on behalf of the owners, and was being watched by Thomas Hobbs. It was Hobbs who identified George as the man who had stolen the deal plank. A local blacksmith James Jenkin, who lived in Halwyn Hill, was called as a character witness, having known George of over 20 years. Clearly, his evidence that George was an "excellent character", and his provision of an alibi, resulted in the jury acquitting him of the charge.

Richard had lived in Crantock all his life and had earned his living as a shoe-maker (cordwainer) until he took over the Miner's Arms around 1840. His wife Mary Ann was also a Crantock resident and together they had eight children before Mary Ann died in 1843 aged 52. In fact, the year after the theft trial, George remarried to another local girl, Ann Polkinhorne, who was over twenty years his junior and had been a servant to William Martyn at Langorrac. It seems that George and his new wife left Crantock soon afterwards and moved to Cubert; perhaps the theft case and remarriage had been too much for them!

The entire cargo from the ship was auctioned by Bernard Hall & Co on 22nd March 1848 on Crantock Beach. The list of timber was: 14,800 Pine Deals, 2,908 pieces Standard Staves and 2,420 West Indian Puncheon Staves.

These latter barrel staves were specifically imported for Liverpool coopers.

The beached hulk of the ship was sold to the Tredwens of Padstow and, on Thursday 3 February, under the supervision of Richard Tredwen she was successfully, and surprisingly, refloated and taken to Padstow for repair. Tredwens was a significant family ship building and repair business based in Padstow that employed around thirty-five men. Richard, and his wife Elizabeth and son Richard, lived in what is now the Cross House Hotel.

So, on 3rd Feb, the ship that had been expected to become a total wreck had been saved. In July, a notice appeared in the Royal Cornwall Gazette advising that the "splendid Vessel", having undergone extensive repairs and refitting, was going to voyage from Padstow to Quebec. Whilst offering general passage for people wishing to emigrate, specific mention was made for any Surgeon wishing to make the passage.

Whilst the Marchioness of Abercorn must have finally set sail from Padstow with Cornish emigrants at the beginning of August, her bad fortune continued because she was back in Falmouth by 25 August after losing her main-top-mast! However, she set sail again on Sunday 3 September with a party of emigrants bound for Quebec where she finally arrived on 5 October. A ship that had been "written off" just ten months earlier was back at sea. And she resumed her Quebec to UK routine.

Unfortunately, her days were numbered and The Marchioness of Abercorn, still owned by the Tredwen family in Padstow, finally ran out of luck at around ten o'clock on the night of 18 November, 1849 when she ran aground between Sheep and Mizen Heads in County Cork. She was on passage from Quebec to Cardiff with a crew of thirty, under Edwin Key, carrying a cargo of timber. Edwin was a 35 year old Padstow man whose family lived in Church Street. Eight of the crew took to a long-boat and succeeded in reaching Rock Island lighthouse and the remainder scrambled off onto the rocks without any loss. The hull, rigging, sails and cargo were auctioned over two days (11 and 12 December) at Crookhaven and at the scene of the wreck on Mizen Head.

The final chapter in the life of a very busy sailing ship closed almost exactly 2 years after she was beached in Crantock.

CHAPTER 3

Farmer William Johns

Willam Johns was born in Crantock in June 1774 to parents Richard and Gertrude. As was common in those days, William had many siblings including Margaret (1767), Thomas (1768), Gertrude (1771), John (1775) and Anne (1779). Thomas died as a teenager. As the eldest surviving son, William eventually inherited his father's farm in the centre of Crantock village and John moved to Trevelveth, now, Trevella farm.

in December 1797, at the age of twenty-three, William married Jane Lawer (sometimes Lower) at Perranzabuloe church. Jane was the daughter of a Cubert family and was five years younger than her husband William. These two went on to have seventeen children, although several died in infancy. By 1812, William and Jane had eight children, including Richard, who would later take over the farm, Jane, who had an "interesting" life described elsewhere, William who would go on to become a mariner and Thomas who rose to a senior position in Cornish banking.

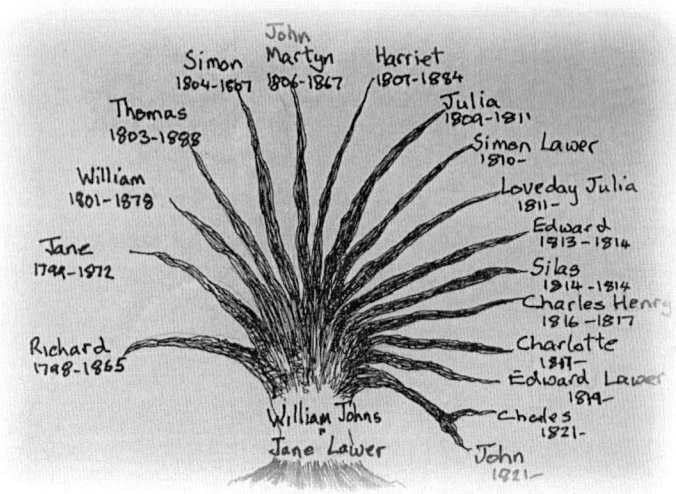

In September 1812, William and Jane suffered a major disaster when a spark from the smithy next to their farm set fire to the barns that were full of corn, straw and hay from the harvest that had only just been completed. The fire was so intense that there were serious concerns that it would envelope the whole village as the majority of the houses were, at that time thatched. The locals had to cover the thatched buildings with winnowing sheets (tarpaulins) that they kept dousing with water to prevent ignition. In the end, William lost his entire store of corn, straw and hay. The smithy and the adjoining house were also destroyed and it was estimated that William's losses amounted to £2500 which was a very large sum of money. Unfortunately, the losses were not covered by any form of insurance. Contemporary reports suggested that Jane, who was described as in "a delicate state of health", was not expected to survive the trauma of the event. In fact, she was pregnant again and another son, Edward, was born in May 1813. Many local farms, and parishes across Cornwall, contributed replacement feed and money to support William in the aftermath of the fire.

Sadly, the accident proved too much for William and, in the late 1813 he rented-out the land that he owned in Crantock and moved across Cornwall to Mawnan where he took a fourteen-year lease on Meudon Farm. The farm house was built by Napoleonic prisoners of war and was named after a suburb of Paris. It was part of the Meudon Manor estate that was owned by Elizabeth Fox. Elizabeth was the wife of Robert Were Fox, one of the Quaker Fox family from Falmouth. They had seven sons and three daughters and all of them made significant contributions to Cornwall during the Industrial Revolution. The family wealth was based on their shipping brokerage business and they used their world-wide contacts to establish the gardens at Trebah, Glendurgan and Penjerrick with plants being brought back on the ships that they operated. One of Robert and Elizabeth's sons, another Robert Were Fox, became a leading light in the creation of the Royal Cornwall Polytechnic Society and the British Association for the Advancement of Science. He was an eminent geologist and became a Fellow of the Royal Society. He also acted as an honorary consul in Falmouth for several overseas countries, including the US and Portugal.

The Royal Cornwall Polytechnic was founded in 1832, partly inspired by Robert the younger's children, Barclay, Anna Maria and Caroline, who eventually took up residence at Penjarrick. Robert managed the Perran Foundry at Perranarworthal and was also responsible for a number of inventions associated with measuring the earth's magnetic field. With their father's encouragement, the Society was formed 'To promote the useful and fine arts, to encourage industry, and to elicit the ingenuity of a community distinguished for its mechanical skill'.

The founder members of the Polytechnic were all drawn from the Fox family members, there were lots of them! An early employee of the Polytechnic was Robert Hunt who later went on to become a Fellow of the Royal Society and lead the Mining Institute. This evolved from a Mining Association established in 1858. The Institute founded the Camborne Laboratory as well as the Redruth, Camborne and Penzance Mining Schools.

The range of interests of the Polytechnic is demonstrated by the list of exhibits at the 1860 exhibition, with sections devoted to Mechanical Engineering (that included brick makers, sewing machines, cooking stoves, hydraulic presses, breakwaters, copper tube makers, various mining equipment and a cranium meter for wig makers),

Fine arts, Plain and Fancy Work, Naval Architecture and Natural History. A true Polytechnic in every sense of the word. Indeed, this is believed to have been the first use of the term Polytechnic in Britain.

Shortly after the family moved to Meudon in 1813, a young violinist called Joseph Emidy gave a concert in Truro under the patronage of Viscount Falmouth. Joseph has a very interesting life story and a connection with Crantock because, according to the Crantock Curchwarden's Account Book, he supplied the Crantock Church Orchestra with an instrument and instructions. Joseph was born in Guinea and sold as a slave to Portuguese traders who sent him to Brazil and later to Portugal. He must have been an accomplished musician because he played violin with the Lisbon opera company. He was captured in 1795 by the Royal Navy and pressed into service as the ship's fiddler for Admiral Sir Edward Pellew, probably on-board HMS Indefatigable during the Napolionic wars. And there is another intriguing story! Edward Pellew was a Cornishman who ran away to sea when he was fourteen and eventually ended up in the Royal Navy in 1770. He was an extremely successful naval commander and eventually rose to the position of Vice-Admiral of the United Kingdom and awarded many accolades, including being appointed Viscount Exmouth. Amongst his successful campaigns was the bombardment of Algiers in 1816 that eventually led to the defeat of the Barbary pirates. He was also responsible for raising a crew composed almost entirely of Cornish miners that captured a French frigate in 1793 resulting in him being presented to the king.

Emidy remained with Pellew until he was discharged ashore in Falmouth in 1799. He made a living by giving music lessons and he married a local girl, Jane Hutchins, in September 1802. They had eight children, although several of them died relatively young. Joseph became a significant character in the local community and gave many concerts in Falmouth. There appears to have been a number of black families in the port and Joseph was witness for the marriage between John Rodney, a black mariner, and Elizabeth Stotten, daughter of a black resident, in 1804.

Emidy's concerts in Falmouth were held at Wynn's hotel that had been opened in 1780 by Mr de Wynn. The Wynn family had been one of those that had benefited from the redistribution of Crantock's church lands after the reformation. By the time that the Johns family moved to Meudon, the hotel was a notable building on the Falmouth seafront in Church street. The building still exists and is recognisable by the two very large bow windows. The hotel was a prominent part of the nautical scene in Falmouth and was often used as an auction room for the sale of ships and their cargoes. In 1808 two cargoes were auctioned that had been captured by armed schooners (privateers) operating from the port. The manifests included 156 hogsheads of red wine and 250 cases of claret seized from an American ship travelling from Bordeaux to New Orleans. There were also animal hides from Lisbon. Falmouth was a primary shipping port at the beginning of the nineteenth century with packet ships travelling all over the globe.

Emidy remained in Falmouth until around 1815 when he, and his expanded family, moved to Truro where he remained until his death in April 1835. While in Truro he founded the Truro philharmonic orchestra, the first such orchestra outside London. He also performed his own compositions and is considered to have been the first black composer in the UK. Whilst he was patronised by the wealthy Cornish community, he never travelled to London and the whereabouts of his compositions is now lost, no records exist of any of his music.

Having moved to Meudon, the Johns family continued to have children. Sadly, they lost young Edward soon after arriving but Silas was born in June 1814, followed by Charles Henry in 1816, although he too died soon afterwards. More were to follow and William and Jane also acquired a new neighbour in Meudon Manor when the younger Robert Were Fox married Maria Barclay in 1814 and moved to the manor. Their children would include Barclay and Caroline who wrote journals about their lives and the influential people, such as Thomas Carlyle and John Sterling, within the circle of friends of the Fox family. These were published as the "Memoirs of Old Friends: Caroline Fox of Penjerrick, Cornwall". Barclay's diaries, that detailed his courtship to Jane

Backhouse as well as his trips overseas to France and Italy, were not published until 1979. Barclay was also a major contributor to the development of the Polytechnic and he devoted much of his life to the gardens at Penjerrick.

In 1820, William's eldest daughter, Jane, got married to a Portuguese, Jose Lamanzo (possibly Lorenzo) da Trinidade from Cidadi. Portugal was a country with which many Famouth ships traded, bringing wine, so there were probably a number of shipping agents operating from the town. In fact, the number of Portuguese grew over the coming years as the country was plunged into a civil war between two brothers claiming the throne.

Jane and Josè had a son, Joseph Lorenzo in the following year but he sadly died within a month of his birth and was buried in Mawnan.

While William was living in Meudon, he still retained ownership of land in Crantock, some of which he leased, including, in 1822, a farm and associated land to John Dunstan who was the mayor of Falmouth. From subsequent events it is probable that William was plagued with financial problems throughout his life so the leasing of his Crantock farm to somebody living in Falmouth was probably associated with a debt.

In April, 1824, William made the newspapers when he was involved in the rescue of the schooner *Providence* that was driven ashore at his farm. The *Providence*, under Henry Sanders, was an almost new, Brixham based ship bound for Cardiff when she was caught in a storm off the Helford and driven on to the rocks. The master was so grateful for the assistance provided by William Johns and his workers that he, together with this crew of seven, wrote to the Royal Cornwall Gazette expressing their thanks for the "truly Christian kindness". Not only did William provide accommodation for the crew for around three weeks but he also managed to help save nearly all their stores and belongings although the ship was totally wrecked. The master reported their position had been compromised by "some loose iron nails in the binnacle, which attracted the compass".

William's oldest son, Richard, married Grace Edwards from Mawnan in March 1824. At this time, he transferred most of his interests in Crantock to Richard and in January 1825, he completed the transfer. Richard took charge of all the land and properties as well as livestock, machinery and feedstuff. From contemporary records, the values of some of his livestock in 1825 were: bullocks £213, sheep £142 16s, horses £60 and pigs £13. It highlights what a major loss the fire of 1818 must have been. The land was divided amongst five "tenements" that were valued on an annual rent; House (£23), Sparke's (£28), Clemow (£8), Lutteralls (£96), Stephens (£7) and Great Weston (£38).

The tenement names generally refer to previous owners and they often contained distributed parcels of land rather than a single "block". For instance, "Great Weston" tenement included a house in the centre of Crantock together with land scattered around the parish from Treago to Sandy Close to West Pentire. Some tenements retained their names through several ownership changes, such as Lutterals, but sometimes they would be re-named after the immediate seller. Lutterals was the largest, and possibly the oldest tenement and refers to one of the land owners after the Reformation.

In the Martyn family records, the names of some of the enclosures within each tenement are recorded. However, it was not until the next decade that formal records were established detailing every piece of land within the parish. These formal records make little reference to the term "tenement".

In 1836, the Whig party, under Lord Melbourne, passed the Tithe Commutation Act. This Act was introduced to simplify the settlement of tithes across England & Wales. Tithes were originally introduced in 855 by Æthelwulf, King of Wessex, as an annual tax based on one tenth of all agricultural produce to support the local church and clergy. After the reformation in the 16th century, much of the land held by the church was passed to lay owners who also inherited the right to receive tithes, as well as becoming the recognised land owners. From the tithes collected, the lay owners were obligated to provide funds to secure and maintain a cleric to serve the parish. However, it was noted in the Parochial History of Cornwall (1838 but based on observations by Hals & Tonkin from the late 18th century) that Crantock parish was wholly impropriated to John Buller of Morval *"who only allows a small stipend to the incumbent (at present Mr Warn), by which, together with the parishioners' benevolence, he makes a hard shift to live."*

The collection of tithes led to the construction of tithe barns in which to store the produce and animals delivered by those bound to the tithe owner. However, by the 19th century there was an increasing trend towards replacing produce with an appropriate sum of money that would often be added as a supplement to the rent paid by the tenant. The Tithe Commutation Act was an attempt to regularise the collection of tithes based on a monetary tax rather than through "in kind" produce.

As a result of the Act, a Tithe Commission was established in 1836 under 3 Commissioners; William Balmire (Chair), Thomas Wentworth Buller and Rev. Richard Jones (nominated by the Archbishop of Canterbury). The Act required a detailed understanding of the land ownership and use within every tithe district (these were often different from the parish boundaries). This led to the first accurate set of maps of England (the Tithe Maps) that were linked to written Schedules.

These were created over the period 1837 to 1841. The Schedules identified every parcel of land with a unique reference number (tied to the map), landowner, occupier, state of cultivation (pasture, arable etc.), area and rent (tithe) payable. Three individual copies of the maps and schedules were produced for every tithe district. One copy was lodged with the Commission (a complete set is held in the National Archive), one with the parish (generally held in the local records office) and another with the Diocesan registrar. There are often subtle differences between the three copies of the Tithe maps.

The Crantock "Apportionment of the Rent Charge in-lieu-of-Tithes" was completed on 22 Feb 1840 with a map (1839) surveyed and drawn by Alexander Withers. The Schedule defined Crantock as 2500 acres, with 2350 acres of arable land. The tithe owner was Sir John Buller Yarde Buller of Lupton House, Brixham. He was a descendant of the Buller family from Morval, Looe, which remains, to this day as a Buller family home. The total value of the Crantock tithes was set at £380 and this was based on a standard set of values placed on Wheat (7s ¼ d per bushel), Barley (3s 11 ½ d) and Oats (2s 9d). Richard Johns, William's son, was appointed as the Valuer for the Parish of Crantock.

The 1839 Apportionment map and associated Schedule provide the first clear evidence of the landowners and land occupiers in Crantock. It is useful that the tithe apportionment in 1840 is just 1 year separate from the first census of the parish in 1841. However, as the two activities were unrelated, and for different purposes, it is important that comparisons between the two sets of information be treated with caution.

Back to William and his return to Crantock in 1827 with his family. His time at Meudon had not been good from a financial point of view. The land was poor and the rent was high so that when he left the farm, he was in arrears with his rent and he had borrowed significantly against his Crantock properties. On his return, William did not live in the village, as his son Richard and his family had taken over the farmhouse. With his wife and some of his children, he moved into Tregunnel farm on the other side of the river Gannel and effectively retired. He was no longer the owner of his home, but leased it from William Martyn. From family papers, it seems that William had to re-mortgage his properties on at least three occasions which made unravelling his affairs extremely difficult when he died.

The year after William moved back to the North coast, his wife Jane died at Tregunnel, aged just 51, after having 17 children during their 31 year marriage. William remained at Tregunnel and in the 1841 census he is described as an "independent" living with his youngest son Charles, daughter Charlotte, an older married daughter Jane Trinidade, Elizabeth Lawer (probably his deceased wife's sister) and Silas Martyn.

It appears that William spent the remainder of his life living at Tregunnel until he died in November 1856 at the age of eighty-one. Following his death, the resolution of his will and estate involved a convoluted series of communications between the executors, led by his accountant son Thomas from Falmouth, and the Inland Revenue. William's affairs proved to be extremely convoluted! In fact, poor Thomas was about to enter into four years of correspondence with the Succession department of the Inland revenue office.

Thomas, worked for the Falmouth Savings bank, and it fell to him to settle the accounts of his father's estate. The result ended up as a very long list of debts that he had accrued during his life. He had mortgaged much of his land to his son Richard (£1500) and some in Pentire (£300) to Henry Symonds. He also had bonds worth £800 with his eldest son as well as a long list of "notes in hand" and outstanding bills. In all, he was in debt to around £4000 at the time of his death. Thomas wrote a long letter to the Inland Revenue in 1860 describing the "complicated and embarrassed" state of William's estate. He explained that his father had suffered serious financial losses both through the fire and the failure of the Meudon venture. He also cited the fact that he had a large family, seventeen children in total, of which nine were surviving at the time of his death. These were six sons; Richard, William, Thomas, Edward Lawer, Henry & Charles (twins who had emigrated to Australia) and three daughters; Jane Trindade, Harriet (who would marry Silas Martyn who had taken over Tregunnel) and Charlotte. Each of these children was due some form of annuity under the terms of the wills of both William and his father Richard. Further complication was the fact that William's aunt, Amelia who was a beneficiary under their father's will, was still alive. An extremely complex estate to unravel!

It was to take over four years for Thomas to finally come to an agreement with the Inland Revenue with payment of Succession Duties of £13-15s-10d (£13.8). Whether William had been clever in putting himself in debt to his eldest son as a means of avoiding excessive Duty is not clear. Sadly, for the family it was not the end of the affair as the Inland Revenue were back in pursuit of further duties some twenty years later when other members of the family died and they sought to recover dues from property handed down through the generations from William's father Richard.

What does emerge from all the correspondence and documents relating to William's death is that his son William, the Master Mariner, received very little income from the estate. Indeed, he only appears to have received one quarter of the income (about £1 per year) from two fields, Vugga Close and Gares Hill, both on West Pentire and part of what was known as the Borlase tenement.

William is buried in Crantock churchyard, along with his wife, Jane and his father, Richard, and mother. Although he was a significant landowner in the village, his loss of almost all of his farming assets in the fire of 1812 haunted him for the rest of his life and he died with debts across the parish that would result in the sale of much of his properties, most of which was eventually acquired by William Martyn.

Whilst William left many relatives behind him and his son Richard revived a considerable proportion of his property, within a couple of generations almost all evidence of the Johns family had disappeared from Crantock parish.

CHAPTER 4

Master Mariner William Johns

On the second of March, 1878, William Johns, a retired Master Mariner died at his lodgings in Mylor Bridge. William was 76 and he had been born in Crantock in 1801 to William and Jane Johns who farmed in the village. William had a life that was dominated by the sea from the age of fifteen. It was William, together with two other local seamen, who took part in the rescue of the Marchioness of Abercorne in 1847.

William was born in 1802, the second son of William and Jane Johns. His older brother, Richard was born in 1798 and he would grow up to be, like his father, a farmer in Crantock. In 1803 Richard and William were joined by a brother, Thomas, who was to remain close to William throughout their lives. In the first 15 years of their marriage, William, senior, and Jane produced eight children, some of whom died very young. In fact, the couple had seventeen children before William's mother Jane died in 1828 at the age of 51.

In September 1812, just as Napoleon was entering Moscow, William senior suffered a major catastrophe when a spark from the smithy's forge set fire to his farm buildings. The end result was that William and his entire family decamped to Meuden Farm near Mawnan on the south coast of Cornwall within a year of the fire.

Within four years of moving to Meuden farm, young William, aged just 15, joined his first ship as a Boy Seaman. The ship was the *Fortitude*, a 377ton schooner, owned by Blackett and company, and under a recently appointed Master, Stafford. The *Fortitude* was an old ship having been built twenty years before in Dysart, on the coast of Fife. She is reported as leaving Falmouth in May 1816 bound for Granada in the West Indies. This was probably William's maiden voyage. Quite a baptism for a young Cornish lad who had never left Cornwall.

It has been possible to trace William's sea-going experience from his application for a Master's Certificate that was awarded to him in 1851. Before 1845 there was little regulation of sea-going personnel. However, in 1845, a system of voluntary examinations for Masters and Mates of foreign trade vessels was introduced by the Board of Trade. By 1850, the Marine Act had been passed that made examinations compulsory and Masters and Mates were granted Certificates of Competency. Masters and Mates who were already serving in these roles were allowed exemption from the examinations providing that they could produce evidence of their sea-going experience. As long as the Board of Trade accepted the evidence, these Masters and Mates were awarded Certificates of Service and this is what William eventually achieved.

William only served about a year on the *Fortitude*, trading between London and the West Indies and around the coast of Britain (including Falmouth and Penzance),

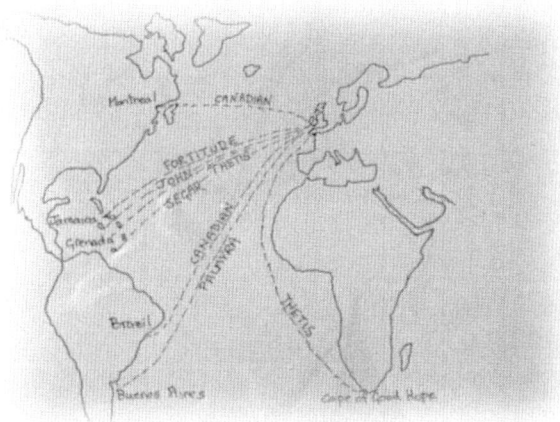

before joining a ship called the *John*, again as a Boy Seaman. Lloyd's Register contains over fifty ships of that name so that it has not been possible to identify his specific ship, although William's Certificate of Service lists her as a 400ton vessel. This was a large vessel for that time and there are only a few examples, all brigs, trading between London and Jamaica, Bristol and Jamaica, Liverpool and Africa and Cowes and the Virgin Islands. A brig generally had two square-rigged masts with a mizzen (fore and aft) sail on the second mast. It is clear that young William, he was only sixteen, was now travelling far from his native Cornwall.

In 1818 William gained promotion to Ordinary Seaman and joined the 187ton (although his Certificate indicates a larger, 250ton ship) brig, the *Palmyra*. The *Palmyra* belonging to Bailey and Company and sailed out of London to various ports including Hamburg and Buenos Aires under her Master, Peters. In 1818 she is listed as sailing from Falmouth in September of that year so perhaps William was able to spend some time at home with his family at Meuden.

In 1813, a ship under the name *Palmyra* was involved in an incident in Guernsey that was key to a major conspiracy trial in the High Court. Bogle, French and company, had been a successful trading business at the beginning of the nineteenth century. However, the company failed in 1806 after losing a number of contracts, one of which was with the Admiralty for the supply of provisions. The company reappeared in 1812, under the ownership of Nathaniel Bogle French (who was a Director of the Bank of England), Augustin Bogle French, and Mr. Barton. The company was still in considerable financial difficulties and, it appears, that the owners decided to resort to piracy in order to solve their problems. They acquired a ship, the *Pitt* (with a declared owner Augustine Bogle French), that they fraudulently transferred to Spanish ownership in order to gain Spanish letters of marque allowing it to operate as an armed privateer under the name *San Juan Baptista*.

In June 1813, the *San Juan* sailed into Guernsey under a Spanish flag which resulted in her being visited by the Spanish consul. He was surprised to find two Englishmen on board, Burke and Welch, who claimed to be merely passengers. The port authorities of Guernsey were suspicious of the ship because Burke and Welch were making enquiries about all the ships in the port and whether they were trading under the British licensing scheme. This scheme allowed vessels to trade legitimately between Britain and mainland Europe, including France. To test their concerns about the *San Juan*, a trap was devised in which the *Palmyra*, sailing under licence for France, set to sea. Within a short time, Burke and Welch went out to the *San Juan* with a pilot and also set sail, apparently in pursuit of the *Palmyra*. Having seen the response, the *Palmyra* turned around and headed back into port. Again, followed by the *San Juan*. On their return, the two British men were summoned before the governor, Sir John Doyle, and asked to explain their actions. Burke boasted that the

British had no jurisdiction over the *San Juan* as it was a Spanish ship and that it was entitled to take any British ship, whether or not they claimed to be sailing under licence. The governor backed down under this argument and both Burke and Welch were released, whereupon they set sail and travelled to Dartmouth. Within a few days both returned to the *San Juan* and proceeded to cruise along the channel near Le Havre. It was during this time that a naval cutter, *Dwarf*, under Captain Gordon, observed the *San Juan* and, as she was flying a Spanish flag, he boarded her to establish its purpose. Burke and Welch remained hidden while he was questioning the Spanish crew and Master, Llosa. As Gordon went below he literally bumped into Welch who again made boast that, as his ship carried a Spanish commission, he was able to take any vessel he met. The following day, the naval captain noticed that the *San Juan* remained on-station off Le Havre and he again boarded the ship and demanded to know their business. He then asserted that he would escort the *San Juan* back to Dover. To this, Welch threatened to withdraw all hands from deck and leave Captain Gordon in command, with the intention that he would sue the Captain for £30,000 damages. The naval captain backed down and left the ship but remained on watch.

Soon afterwards, a Danish ship the *Carlotta*, came into sight and the naval cutter boarded her and inspected her papers that confirmed that she was sailing under licence from London to Le Havre. As Captain Gordon watched, the *San Juan* gave chase to the *Carlotta*, stopped and boarded her with an armed crew. Captain Gordon agreed to offer escort of the *Carlotta* back to Portsmouth, probably hoping to share the prize! In the end the naval ship withdrew and the *San Juan* docked in Portsmouth alone with the *Carlotta*, now being sailed by a Spanish crew. The intention was to leave Portsmouth and return to a Spanish port but the Admiralty impounded the ship and refused to let her sail. Burke and Welch challenged this action, stating that she was a Spanish ship with a Spanish crew and under a Spanish captain. They travelled to Spain on several occasions to try to get support for their claim but to no effect.

Bogle French and company continued to be in financial difficulties but with the capture of the *Coletta*, the company continued to trade under promises of recovering £30,000 owed to their creditors from the sale of the goods aboard the ship. Unfortunately, they were declared bankrupt before they could resolve the impounding of the *Coletta* and thus gain the £30,000 that would have rescued them. At their bankruptcy hearing in May 1815, it was revealed that they actually owed in excess of £100,000. Sadly, for them, on the day that they were declared bankrupt, the Spanish authorities agreed to fight their case with the Admiralty for the release of the ship. Too late!

In 1817, Augustin Bogle French, John Barton, John French Burke, Matthew Welch, and Joze Antonio de la Llosa (although as a Spanish national never brought to trial), were charged with conspiring, together with Nathaniel Bogle French deceased, and with other persons unknown, on the 1st December, 1812, to seize, detain and capture the *Coletta* navigating under the protection of licences granted in pursuance of an Act of Parliament.

The case was initially heard in London before the Court of King's bench in December 1818. It was a very long and convoluted trial during which it was confirmed that Bogle French and company had been complicit in the affair and that Burke and Walch had been in their pay throughout. It was also proven that the sale of the *Pitt* to Spain was fraudulent and that, again, Burke had acted as a paid agent. The ship had remained British property throughout the exercise and was thus guilty of taking the Danish ship that was sailing under licence to carry goods.

The trial concluded in 1819 with Burke being sentenced to three years in prison and Augustine Bogle French and Welch to eighteen months each.

William Johns left the *Palmyra* in the year of this case and joined a new ship *Speedy,* remaining as an Ordinary Seaman. His Certificate identifies this as a 248 ton ship. As with the *John*, it is not possible to be definitive about this ship as there are numerous ships named *Speedy* in Lloyd's Register. The most likely candidate is a 175ton brig, owned by Sutherland & Co, that was listed as trading out of Falmouth. William only stayed on this ship for a short time before leaving and gaining promotion to Second Mate on board the *Victoria* (250ton). Again, the precise identification of this ship is not possible as there are at several ships called *"Victoria"* of around 250tons at this time.

In 1822, at the age of 21, William rose to the rank of Chief Mate aboard a ship called *Canadian*. She was a 263ton snow rigged ship. The snow rig carried two square rigged foremasts with a mizzen stepped immediately behind the second mast. The *Canadian* was owned by Miller & company and sailed between Liverpool and Brazil and Liverpool and Montreal. Her Master over the time William served was called Udney. The *Canadian* had been built in Montreal in 1822 so that she was a brand-new ship when William joined her.

In 1823, the *Canadian* was trading mostly with South America from Liverpool with voyages to Pernambuco in Brazil and Darien in Panama. In July, 1823, on return from Darien, she landed around one thousand bales of cotton at Prince's dock in Liverpool, together with twenty-two tierces and forty-two half-tierces of rice. A tierce was a measure of volume equivalent to about 25 gallons. In 1824 the ship voyaged exclusively between Liverpool and Canada with trips to Quebec and her home port of Montreal. It is likely that all of these voyages were to bring back timber to feed the expanding building programmes of the North-West.

William left the *Canadian* in 1824 and joined the *Thetis*, a 340 ton schooner owned by George Joad & Co. William remained in the rank of Chief Mate. This was a very old ship, over 30 years old, that had been built on the Thames. She traded exclusively between London and the Cape of Good Hope and Jamaica although there are no records of her cargo. It is known that George Joad, who was based in Blackheath, was a ship-owner who had numerous connections with Jamaican Plantations (specifically Anchovy Bottom and Mount Zion). He had invested in these plantations and thus became a creditor when London based sugar merchant, John Plummer and William Wilson were declared bankrupt in 1830.

Although the slave trade had been abolished in 1808, it was not until 1834 that slavery itself was abolished. In the intervening years, there were as many as 300,000 slaves working on the plantations in Jamaica and in 1831 there was a major uprising called the Baptist war (it was initiated by an enslaved Baptist minister) in which around 60,000 slaves were involved. The British troops quelled the uprising and several hundred slaves were either killed or executed for petty crimes. The ending of the slave trade resulted in plantation owners having to pay workers to harvest their crops. This made Jamaican sugar uncompetitive with other regions such as the southern states of America and is probably the reason for the bankruptcy of Plummer and Wilson.

The *Thetis* was finally decommissioned around 1825/26 and her last recorded sailing was in 1825 when she is listed as leaving Liverpool for Cardigan with a cargo of "soap-waste". A sad end to a ship that had traded all over the Atlantic sea-board for most of its life.

In 1825, probably as the *Thetis* was pensioned off, William joined the Topsham built, *Segar* (sometimes *Seagar*), another snow-rigged ship. She was also quite old, seventeen, and was again owned by George Joad for shipping between London and Jamaica. William's time on the *Segar* was cut short when she was wrecked on the North-East coast of an island called Great Heneage whilst returning from Jamaica to London under her master Powell on 14 September 1826. All survived and some of the cargo was saved by an American schooner, the *Mount Vernon* that took the crew to Baltimore. News of the wrecking was brought back to Falmouth by the packet ship *Lady Mary Pelham* on the 24th, no doubt the news of William's rescue was relayed to the Johns family at Meudon.

The island of Great Heneage is only about 55 miles long and 20 miles wide. It had been surveyed in 1799 by a naval sloop, *Stork*, and is situated at the southern end of the Bahamas. Great Heneage claimed many ships on passage from Jamaica, including two Naval vessels, *HMS Lowestoffe* (1801) and *HMS Statia* (1815). The *Lowestoffe* was a frigate, built in 1760, that saw service in the seven-year war before being stationed in the

Caribbean for four years. In 1777 the ship was extensively overhauled in Britain before returning to the Leeward Islands in the Caribbean. Two officers who served on her during this commission were Horatio Nelson and Cuthbert Collingwood, who formed a friendship that would last until Nelson's death at Trafalgar. Over the next four years *Lowestoffe* was involved in a number of successful actions associated with the American War of Independence. Between 1783 and 1785 she was again refitted and returned to service in the channel and Mediterranean where she was involved with a number of successful actions against the French. At the end of the eighteenth century the *Lowestoffe* returned to convoy duty in the West Indies. It was during a convoy that she was eventually wrecked on Little Heneage, along with a number of merchant ships, when an unexpectedly strong current swept them off course while trying to transit from Jamaica. At the subsequent court-martial in Port Royal, her Captain, Robert Plampin, was exonerated and he went on to achieve the rank of Vice-Admiral and was the commander of St Helena when Napoleon Bonaparte was imprisoned there in 1816.

Today the island of Great Heneage is known as Great Inagua, its original name was of Spanish origin and meant "water can be found". It has a significant sea salt business that dates back to the seventeenth century but it is also home to a large bird sanctuary (flamingos) and nature reserve. There are around nine hundred permanent residents. Together with its small sister island, Little Heneage, the island has a history of association with Caribbean piracy with claims that gold treasure was buried in the 16th and 17th centuries. However, by the time that William was ship-wrecked, piracy had all but disappeared. The last West Indian pirate, Roberto Cofresi, was captured and executed in Puerto Rico in 1825, the year before the loss of the *Segar*.

There now follows a gap in the career of William as his Certificate of Competency indicates that he did not go back to sea for a further twelve years, at the age of thirty-seven. In 1838 he is listed as the co-owner and Master of a new ship called the *Liberty*. She was a much smaller ship than those on which William had served most of his life. The *Liberty* was built in 1838 in Ilfracombe by Harris & Challson. Lloyd's Register describes her as a 47 ton smack built of English oak and elm with a single mast. She was surveyed by Lloyd's in September 1838 in Newport, probably following her maiden voyage from Ilfracombe. Her home port was given as Padstow.

The *Liberty* joined a fleet of small trading vessels that operated around the coast of Cornwall. These vessels were used to transport a wide range of cargo, such as lime, coal and mineral ore, between the major ports, including Padstow, Falmouth, Penzance, Hayle and Fowey, to the multitude of smaller harbours at Pentewan, Portreath, Newquay (and the Gannel) and almost anywhere that a small ship could be either moored or beached. Cornwall, being surrounded on three "sides" by water was almost unique in developing extensive sea-borne trade rather than using cross-country tracks and roads. It was not until the arrival of the railways in the mid-nineteenth century that the coastal trading reduced.

The *Liberty*, under William, operated around the coasts of the Cornwall, Wales and France throughout her long-life. Like many other ships, she joined the network of traders bringing coal from South Wales and transporting metal ores back to the smelting works in Swansea and Neath.

During her life, the *Liberty* underwent one major alteration in 1851 when a new section was inserted to increase her tonnage to 66. From the census of that year, it is apparent that William was living with his family at Tregunnel, probably waiting for the conversion to complete. After her conversion, the *Liberty* was described as the ugliest ship ever to enter Newquay harbour!

William has been traced through a couple of events that befell him during his time in charge of the *Liberty*. In November 1843, William and his banker brother, Thomas, were badly injured when their gig overturned while travelling from Crantock back to their home in Truro. Thomas sustained a sprained wrist but William was more seriously injured with a broken arm and leg as well as two broken ribs that no doubt would have kept him shore-bound for some time. It was reported that he was recovering at his home in Fairmantle street, Truro.

Thomas was born in Crantock in April 1803 and moved to Mawnan with his parents in 1812. He clearly chose a career in accountancy as he is listed in the 1841, '51, '61, '71 and 1881 census records for Falmouth in this profession. According to both the 1841 and 1851 censuses he lived in Arwenack street, as an accountant. He was actually appointed as Actuary to The Falmouth Savings Bank in February 1846 replacing the late Mr Joseph Earle. This bank was founded in 1817 and from 1833 it had offices on the first floor of the Royal Cornwall Polytechnic Society Hall at 24 Church Street, now occupied by The Poly. In 1861 he had moved to 23 Wodehouse Terrace where he lodged with an annuitant

Elizabeth Lowry, and her sister and husband. He remained as Secretary and Actuary for the Falmouth Savings Bank and the General Statement of Funds states that the bank had 2847 accounts with funds of around £112k. In 1871 Thomas is listed as the head, and only resident at Wodehouse Terrace and is described as an Accountant and Landowner, presumably after the estate of his father had finally been settled. He remains in Wodehouse Terrace in 1881, although by this time he is listed as retired. Thomas died in Falmouth in 1888 and he was buried in Crantock churchyard.

William reappears in the press in 1847 for his part in saving the crew of the Marchioness of Abercorn when she was driven ashore near Vugga cove in a gale on 8 Dec 1847. Although 3 people were drowned, over 20 were saved after three men rowed out through the surf to attach a line to the ship. The heroism of the local mariners was recognized in the following year by the award of RNLI silver medals to William Darke, William Found and William Johns. All three were mariners attached to different ships. The fact that all three were associated with different vessels indicates just how busy Crantock (and specifically the river Gannel) was in the mid-nineteenth century in terms of shipping. William Darke was the master of a new 70 ton schooner, Rose, that had been built in Padstow for Michell & Co who traded around the Cornish Coast. Two weeks after the rescue, William Darke married Phillippa, the daughter of the Chief Officer of the Coast Guard, David Llewelyn from Newquay.

But back to William Johns and his ship *Liberty*. After her conversion in 1851, the *Liberty* continued to trade on the same routes as before until she disappears from Lloyd's Register in 1869 when she would have been 31 years old and William would have been 68. William retired to Mylor Bridge at around this time and in the census of 1871 he is recorded as living as a lodger. William's father, William, died in Crantock in 1856 and Mariner William inherited a very small portion of the estate compared to his eight living relatives. The majority of his father's estate was equally divided amongst all his other children, but mariner William only inherited one quarter of a small packet of land on West Pentire between Vugga Cove and Pusey steps below the current C-Bay. There is no explanation in the correspondence around the distribution of William's estate as to why his namesake son received so little.

The *Liberty* carried on sailing after William retired (but now "out of classification") and was based in Newquay. On 31 January, 1871, under a new captain Howse (almost certainly House?), she came across a derelict schooner (well apart from the dog!), the *Glenfeaden*, loaded with copper ore. She was a Portreath ship that traded between Cornwall and the South Wales ports carrying ore and coal – like the *Liberty*. Portreath had been the premier port for the export of copper ores to South

Wales and the import of coal for the steam engines. By 1840, over 100,000 tons of ore were shipped and the "Welsh Fleet" operated over 700 shiploads/year. The *Glenfeaden* was a schooner of 128 tons and it transpired that she had collided with a barque, the *J H Hea*. All the crew had been taken aboard the barque. There was a subsequent board of enquiry at which the *J H Hea* was held entirely responsible for the collision. There were also claims for salvage with the *Liberty* receiving £75.

Liberty made a habit of rescuing abandoned ships because in March of the following year she found the three-masted, 201 ton schooner *Leader* on her beam-ends with no crew left on board. *Liberty* managed to tow the *Leader* across the Bristol channel to Ilfracombe. It transpired that the crew had all been taken off when the cargo had shifted and taken to Llanelly. The ship (that was only 5 years old and registered in Garmouth. Scotland) appears to have been saved.

In 1883 *Liberty* was owned by Albert J Carter, of Pentewan and in 1887 by Wm H. Bate. In 1891 she was registered as a ketch still under his ownership. She was sold as a ketch at Swansea and her register closes on March 16th 1905 – aged 67!

William died in 1878, so his ship out-lived him, and he was buried in Mylor. It is surprising that William did not return to live with the family in Crantock or even move in with his brother Thomas in Falmouth. In 1871, both Jane and Charlotte were still living in the Crantock, although by then they had moved in with their nephew William Martyn, a farmer in Churchtown. William's brother, Thomas lived a further ten years and died in 1888. He was buried in Crantock churchyard (even though he appears to have lived most of his life in Falmouth) with a headstone that commemorates both him and his brother William.

William's sea-going career was probably similar to many Cornish mariners although he is perhaps unusual in that he served even his early years on large ships on global routes rather than cutting his teeth in the flotilla of small coastal trading vessels. There is also the mystery of his "missing years" between being ship-wrecking in the *Segar* as a Chief Mate in 1826 and his return as Master and Owner of the small coastal *Liberty* in 1938. It was common in this time for local mariners to escape their impoverished upbringings by working their way up through the ranks to Master and possibly co-owner before retiring in relative affluence. Many of the Cornish ports have examples of substantial properties being built by retiring Master Mariners but William died as a lodger in a small cottage in Mylor Bridge with a very small income from the inheritance from his father. Why, and was it linked to his twelve-year disappearance?

CHAPTER 5

Jane Johns – The Lady of Mystery

Jane Gertrude Johns was born to William and Jane Johns in Crantock in 1799. After the disastrous fire in 1812, that destroyed her father's farming business, she moved with the family to Meudon Barton, Mawnan in 1813. The family became a part of the Falmouth community and on 25 July 1821, Jane married a Portugese man and, three years later, her elder brother Richard married local girl Grace Edwards. Further, her younger brothers, Thomas joined the Falmouth Savings Bank and William went to sea on a Falmouth based ship.

Jane's husband was José Lamanzo da Trinidade. He came from Evora Cidadi in central Portugal. It is interesting that the marriage was not witnessed by any close members of the family, although one of them was a Martyn. It appears to have been a "rushed" affair (with a special license) and there are even suggestions that José was already married, or maybe Jane was pregnant.

Little is known about José, but the speculation is that he was either associated with the wine trade or else that he was a mariner. Certainly, Falmouth was at the heart of the Portuguese wine importation business and was a very active port at this time. There is one reference to a Captain Trinidade in 1835 when his ship, the Felis Pensamenti, had off-loaded a cargo in Bristol. The

Captain was paid £50 in notes of the Bristol Old Bank that he stowed in a cupboard in his cabin. The next day he discovered that his money had been eaten by rats. Apparently the ship was infested with rats. However, the bank was very understanding and repaid the Captain in gold sovereigns. Whether this was Jane's husband or not, we will never know.

José and Jane Trinidade stayed in the Mawnan area after their marriage and on 18th June, 1822 it is recorded that a son (Joseph Lorenzo da Trindade) was buried in Mawnan, aged just 1 month. This is the last definitive record that has been found relating to Jane and her husband until 1841 when the first census of Cornwall was published. This identifies that her father, William, aged 65 has moved back to the North coast at Tregunnel with Jane Trinidade (aged 40) listed as a married daughter along with other children and relatives.

The unanswered question is what happened in the nineteen years between 1822 and 1841?

The family legend, supported by local folklore, is that José and Jane travelled abroad after they lost the baby. While on their travels, José either sold Jane, or they were captured by Barbary pirates and eventually Jane found her way to a Moroccan (or Algerian) harem where she was kept prisoner as a concubine. There are even some suggestions that she was taken to the Caribbean but they may be based on her husband's name being confused with Trinidad. The story continues that Jane, somehow, managed to get word from her prison to some sailors from Bristol who brought news back to Cornwall. Her brother, Thomas (actually it is far more likely that it was William) sailed out and rescued her after she had escaped from the harem in a barrel and was smuggled to his ship. He then brought her home to Crantock where she landed in secret. Some versions say that she gave birth to a baby on her return, but it only survived a few days.

The censuses from 1841, '51, '61 and '71 identify that Jane was living in Crantock parish until she died in 1872 at the age of 72. There is a surviving photograph of her. She never spoke of her adventure to anybody and so the story was never recorded. There is some jewellery that she is understood to have brought back with her, a jug and a clay pipe that was supposedly being smoked by her guard at the time of her escape. There are no stories about what might have happened to her husband José.

From official documents, it is also known that her brother William had a new ship built, in 1838 in Ilfracombe. The ship was a smack, christened *"Liberty"*, supposedly to commemorate her safe return to Crantock. Lloyd's Register identifies that the ship was owned by "Captain & Co", but there are no records of who else may have been part-owners.

But can the stories of Jane's disappearance be true? There are virtually no primary sources to verify what happened in the nineteen years between 1822 to 1841. We do know that her family returned to Crantock parish in 1827 and that Jane's mother died in 1828 at the age of 51. She was buried in Crantock churchyard.

First, there is the connection to Portugal. In the eighteenth century, there was a flourishing trade between Britain and Portugal and there was a regular Packet ship service established between Falmouth and Lisbon. The Packets were vessels that operated on behalf of the Post Office to carry letters and packages around the world. Packet ships were privately owned, but built to Post Office specifications, and armed. They were paid for by the Post Office but could earn extra revenue by taking passengers (and gold). In 1830, it would cost sixteen guineas for a cabin and eight guineas for steerage to Lisbon. The Lisbon packet would leave Falmouth every Friday. There were also regular sailings between Falmouth and the Portuguese colony of Brazil with a cabin costing £73.

The Packet ships are known to have taken advantage of the fact that they were seldom stopped and searched by the Royal Navy so they were able to act as transports (smugglers) for British manufactured goods being exported to Portugal, another source of income for the captains. There was a thriving return import business focused on Portuguese wine although the balance of payments was firmly in favour of Britain. This balance was settled with gold that Portugal obtained from their Brazilian colony. Daniel Defoe wrote a definitive account of the way in which the Portuguese-British trade flourished through the Falmouth-Lisbon sea route; first based on the Packet service but later using separate ships owned by the merchants. Vast quantities of gold, perhaps direct from Brazil, would be landed in Falmouth and transported by road to London. It is not surprising that there was an established community of Portuguese traders in and around Falmouth dealing in a wide range of goods, including wines, at the time when the Johns family moved to Meudon.

Portugal was subject to considerable turmoil at the beginning of the nineteenth century. It was invaded by the French allied with Spain, in 1807 after it refused to support an embargo on British goods. The Portuguese Court moved to its overseas colony of Brazil and Rio de Janeiro became a remote "capital of Portugal". The French, who also took over their ally Spain, were ejected from Portugal during the Peninsula War by a coalition led by the British army, under Arthur Wellesley (later Duke of Wellington). Portugal became the base from which the British invaded Spain and eventually France. After the battle of Waterloo in 1815, Portugal remained in a state of instability and an uprising in Oporto in 1821 resulted in the return of the Court from Brazil. The first Portuguese constitution under João VI was established the following year, 1822. It did not last! João's Spanish wife did not agree with his new liberal approach and supported their youngest son to lead a rebellion against her husband, his father. In 1823, the constitution was suspended under the son, Miguel and the country returned to an absolute monarchy. Brazil declared independence from Portugal in 1825 with Miguel's older brother Pedro as Emperor. Again, it did not last!

In 1826, Portugal became embroiled in a conflict between the two brothers; Miguel and Pedro. It is a convoluted story but Pedro having chosen to be Emperor of Brazil, nominated his seven-year old daughter Maria as the Queen of Portugal. His brother Miguel argued that his older brother had relinquished any right to the throne and thus declared himself king of Portugal and a bloody civil war ensued. At the beginning, Miguel rapidly took control of large areas of the country and its close dependencies such as Madeira.

Hundreds of refugees arrived in Falmouth from Portugal. In September 1828 at least 1,000 arrived in the port. This was a huge influx as the population of Falmouth at this time was only around 7,500 people. Further, in the previous month over 500 Germans had disembarked on voyage to America and then refused to re-join their ships! Also in 1828, several British merchants were arrested in Oporto and Lisbon and either deported or imprisoned. This was no little "skirmish". By October of 1828, 125 prisoners had been charged with offences against the "pretender to the throne" and over 80 had been executed. 139 people were killed in a battle for one of the Azores islands and it was estimated that over 50,000 people had "disappeared" on mainland Portugal, either imprisoned, murdered or had fled the country.

The British government, under Prime Minister Arthur Wellesley (later the Duke of Wellington), initially backed Miguel but by 1828 the government had changed allegiance and allowed the child queen Maria, who was still barely ten years old, to land in Falmouth in September 1828 aboard a Brazilian frigate. She was greeted by British diplomats and the Fox family (who acted as Consuls for many overseas nations) as the rightful queen of Portugal. Contemporary reports describe a very impressive reception with lots of local children and militia to greet the queen. She was paraded to Truro and thence to Exeter, Bath and finally London where she was received by the Prime Minister and the king, George IV – who was just recovering from a particularly nasty attack of gout.

In 1829, there was a growing resistance movement in Portugal with guerrilla action in Northern Portugal with troops recruited from Denmark, Netherlands and British Portuguese emigrants. This is the first recorded instance of the use of the term guerrilla fighting. These guerrilla forces attracted more support from the native Portuguese and Pedro relinquished the title of Emperor of Brazil (in favour of his son, Maria's brother) and returned to Portugal in 1831 to lead the resistance to his brother. Eventually, Pedro and the infant queen's army defeated Miguel who surrendered in 1834 at Evora, interestingly, José Trindade's birthplace. Miguel was exiled and Maria, at the age of fifteen, was crowned Queen Maria II. She died during child-birth (she had eleven difficult pregnancies!) when she was only thirty-four but she was well loved by the Portuguese who christened her the Good Mother.

Falmouth and Lisbon were very closely attached by trade during the early nineteenth century. It is also apparent that many Portuguese fled the country when the French invaded in 1808 and it seems eminently likely that some of these would have landed in Falmouth. The Cornish newspapers of this period carried weekly bulletins on the events as they unfurled in Portugal during the 1820s and 1830s, when Jane and José met and married. Much of the intelligence about the events in Portugal came from the Packet ship captains that were travelling to and fro. The timing of José and Jane's wedding in 1821 coincides with the point at which João VI returned from Brazil and established the first parliament. Is it possible that José was a supporter of João and took the opportunity of his return from exile in Brazil to go back to Portugal with his Cornish wife? If that was the case, it seems likely that they would have become embroiled in the subsequent activities as João was usurped by Miguel who was then defeated by his brother Pedro. Was it a coincidence that the final actions of the civil war occurred at Evora where José was born?

Next, we should examine the story that Jane was abducted by, or sold to, Barbary pirates by her husband. Barbary covers the current day countries of Morocco, Tunisia, Algeria and Libya. The Barbary pirates were at their height in the previous centuries. In the 17th and 18th Centuries, the Barbary Corsairs created havoc around the Atlantic seaboard. They attacked towns and villages, captured fishing boats and merchantmen and abducted hundreds of Christians to work as slaves in the Barbary states. The Salé Rangers from Morocco were amongst the most fearsome and in the 17th century they were responsible for many raids along the Cornish coast such as those at Looe, Fowey and Newlyn. At their height, it has been estimated that the Barbary pirates seized over 1,500 people annually from the South West.

By the start of the 19th century, their influence had been considerably reduced. The United States had been a major factor in this by deciding to use naval force to ensure safe passage for its merchant shipping into the Mediterranean rather than pay the "protection" money demanded by the corsairs. It has been quoted that the US were paying the corsairs over $500,000 in the 1790's. The US, in conjunction with a number of European countries, fought two wars against the Barbary pirates, first in 1801 and again in 1815.

In 1816, under further pressure from Britain, Tunis and Tripoli abolished slavery of Christians, but Algiers refused to follow suit. The British sent a large fleet under Admiral Sir Edward Pellew to demand that Algiers stop their slave trading. The action was prompted by the massacre of innocent white slaves the previous year. A stand-off resulted that was settled when the British fleet attacked. Algiers capitulated within 12 hours after it was almost totally destroyed by the bombardment of over 50,000 cannon balls and 1000 shells that left over 2000 dead. In fact, the British fleet also suffered significant losses and damage to the blockading ships. After this action, the Barbary pirates activities were significantly reduced, although they were not completely eradicated until the French invaded in 1830.

So, by the time Jane disappeared around 1822 to be held by Barbary pirates, their influence was almost completely spent and the white slave trade had virtually disappeared in the Western Mediterranean. And, if she was held, could she have escaped so easily? Even that is questionable when considering some of the atrocities that happened to the women in harems in the Eastern Mediterranean. One example was the Albanian harem of the notorious Ali Pasha. Any of his women that were sighted by an outsider would be ruthlessly killed. Indeed, during one episode when some of his enemies managed to breach the harem's defences, he took all the women who had been seen, put them in sacks and had them thrown into the sea to drown.

So, if Jane remained near the Atlantic seaboard it is very unlikely that she could have been abducted and surely it would have been sufficiently unusual for it to have made the newspapers but, after much research, not a trace has been found.

There is also another possible connection between Jane and her Master Mariner brother William. It is a matter of fact that William served on board numerous large ships that traded to the West Indies, one of the last refuges for pirates, and indeed, his last trip as a sailor ended in ship-wreck close to islands that were closely associated with piracy. There is then the lost time in William's sea-going record between 1826 and the purchase of the *Liberty* in 1838.

There is a very large quantity of documentation relating to the winding up of the estate of Jane's father, William Johns, in 1856. This includes a long letter between Jane's brother, Thomas, and the Inland Revenue describing all the misfortunes that befell William and led to his debts and enforced moves between Crantock, Mawnan and back again, but no suggestion that Jane had been another source of concern. Indeed, his will treats all of his surviving children similarly, although Richard did inherit his properties and Master Mariner William barely gets a mention (but perhaps his ship had been financed by the family?).

There is one final twist to this story. In 1917, the famous Cornish author, Sir Arthur Quiller-Couch (Q) published a novel "Aunt Trindad"! This book describes the telling of a story to Seraphim Johns by his Godmother (Hannah Trudgian – who was also known as Aunt Trinidad) and two of her friends (Ann Bonney and Jane Raidlaw). In the story, a pirate Philip Marie Coster (half Portuguese) living on the isle of Tortuga (Haiti) sends a Frenchman Raymond de Noc to find him a wife. Raymond captures Hannah and they fall in love. However, he takes her back to Tortuga and presents her to the pirate in his stronghold. Hannah refuses to marry the pirate so she is thrown into a cell inside a tower on top of a cliff and given three days to change her mind. She finds two barrels that she empties and then, in the night, she lowers herself over the cliff and floats on the barrels out to

Raymond who is conveniently waiting in his boat. Unfortunately, a guard spots the boat, opens fire and poor Hannah is left with a dead Raymond. From that day on she is known as Trinidad after the point of land on the island by the fortress. The book goes on to recount many adventures that befall her before she finally gets home to Bristol!

Now, whether Q heard this story, or a relative of Jane's read the story and fitted Jane's life into it we will never know! But it is fascinating that there are so many similarities; pirates, Portuguese, Trinidad, Johns, Jane, Ann, barrels to escape. Surely, too many for it to be a mere coincidence!

The whole story of Jane Trinidade will probably never be unearthed. As we close off one possibility, another opens.

Jane died in Crantock on 14 March 1872 (recorded as Jane Tindale) and was buried in Crantock churchyard near her father and mother as well as her brother Thomas, whose headstone also records the mariner brother William and two uncles. Whilst their gravestones are all clearly visible, Jane's has sadly disappeared.

CHAPTER 6

Crantock and the Industrial Revolution

The Industrial Revolution covers a period from the middle of the 18th to the late 19th Century. It is often divided into 2 phases with the first part, until the 1830's, being totally driven by Britain with its vast global Empire and transformation from a rural economy to a manufacturing and urban society. The second half, that covered the reign of Queen Victoria from 1836 to 1901, saw the innovations created in Britain being exported across Europe and North America. It is sometimes not appreciated what changes occurred over a relatively short-time scale. For example, from Stephenson's rocket in 1829 to the Great Western Railway from London to Bristol by the 1840's with Penzance being reached by 1867.

Britain led the world, spurred on by the rapid growth of the cotton trade, first with the invention of devices such as the spinning jenny and then, with the introduction of steam engines. The steam engine revolutionised mining in Cornwall and Cornwall revolutionised the development of steam powered machinery.

Cornwall was the world's leading source for copper, tin, zinc and lead, all of which were of major importance to the industrial revolution with their uses in creating alloys; bronze, brass and pewter, tin-plating, copper wires, lead batteries etc. It was even a source of iron ore for making steel, undoubtedly the most significant "new" material that transformed the way things were manufactured during the Industrial Revolution.

The two problems with Cornwall and metal mining are water and hard-rock. Over centuries, from the bronze age, metals had been mined in Cornwall. Many of the deposits were "alluvial" (tin ore gravel collected from streams) and simply extracted from rivers flowing off the moors. This led to shallow, often open-cast, mines alongside the rivers. However, as this was exhausted, mines had to burrow deeper into the ground, leading to a need to remove large quantities of water that inevitably flowed into the pits and to drive through the hard granite rocks. Metal ores tend to occur at the boundaries between the hard, metamorphic rocks (granite) and the softer sedimentary rocks. Whilst some of these early mines employed water-wheels, or even animal powered pumps, the depths from which water could be extracted were limited.

In the early 18th Century (1712) Thomas Newcomen built the first simple steam engine – called an atmospheric engine because it effectively only worked using atmospheric pressure whereas a modern steam engine operates at around 20 times these pressures. The Newcomen engines were inefficient and required lots of coal to fire the boiler. Thus, they became widely used in coal-mining regions that could supply the large quantities of fuel required. However, despite their heavy fuel consumption, many of these were built and installed in Cornish mines to pump out deeper shafts. These engines provided early opportunities for Cornish engineers to supply component parts, including boilers, and develop improvements to their design.

In the 1760's, James Watt began to experiment with the Newcomen engine design and he eventually created a far more efficient design, although it still only used very low pressures (just above atmospheric) primarily because the boilers were very crude – little more than big kettles made of copper and lead sitting over a fire.

Watt engines were used across Britain, to power factories and operate in collieries. Because many of these areas were near major deposits of coal, there was little need to improve their fuel consumption and they remained inefficient.

Watt was an engineer, not a businessman, and it took his partnership with Matthew Boulton in the 1770's to see the business really take off. Boulton & Watt patented their steam engines and they succeeded in getting an act of parliament to grant them a monopoly on steam engine designs until 1800. They also ensured that everything that they developed around their steam engine design was patented; devices such as the planet gearing and special linkages that converted up-and-down, linear, to rotary motion. They effectively leased the engines to mine owners and collected fees during their operational terms. They employed "field engineers" and in Cornwall, a Scotsman William Murdoch, who introduced gas street lighting to Redruth, was one of those responsible for maintaining their machines. These "incomer" engineers added to the "home-grown" expertise within Cornwall and invigorated engineering research and development. During this period Cornwall could boast a large number of Fellows of the Royal Society and others who were leading members of the new engineering institutions.

The downside of the patenting of the Watt steam-engine, was that development stalled for over twenty years until their patents expired. Several engineers working in Cornwall, including Jonathon Hornblower and Richard Trevithick, realised that the low-pressure Watt engines were inefficient and could be vastly improved by increasing steam pressure. Hornblower had moved to Cornwall from Stafford in 1744, attracted by the engineering opportunities offered by the many Newcomen engines operating in the mines. He had a brother, Josiah, who went to New Jersey in 1753 to erect the first steam engine (a Newcomen design) in the New World. The sea crossing was so bad that Josiah vowed never to go on a ship again and he remained in America for the rest of his life!

In 1781 Hornblower developed a two-cylinder, compound steam engine where the steam passed from a high-pressure cylinder into a second low-pressure cylinder. Watt took legal action and development was stopped until 1803. Trevithick was also a brilliant engineer (and poor businessman). He lived next door to William Murdoch in Redruth and he married the daughter of John Harvey who had established the engineering works in Hayle. Trevithick pioneered high-pressure steam engines, using significant improvements in boiler technology and the use of iron in the structures. Working with another Cornish engineer, Andrew Vivian, Trevithick installed a high-pressure steam engine at a mine in St Agnes in 1797 having won a competition against a low-pressure Watt engine. In celebration, the locals named the two offshore rocks (now known as Man and His Man) as Captain Dick and Captain Andrew.

In Cornwall, there was a far greater emphasis on improving fuel consumption of the early steam engines as all the fuel had to be imported from South Wales. This led to the development of the cylindrical Cornish boiler where flue gases passed through the boiler and then returned underneath. The Cornish boiler led to significant improvements in the efficiency of many Watt engines but it also led to legal challenges that higher pressures infringed the patents. Watt was very concerned about high-pressure steam and the potential for major boiler explosions, of which there were many!

The lapse of Boulton & Watt's monopoly patents, after 1800, witnessed enormous improvements in steam engine performance and efficiency with Trevithick demonstrating the first steam locomotive in 1801. With the wider use of steel, improved boiler and engine designs, pressures began to increase and the fuel efficiency and output power of the engines improved rapidly.

All of these innovations in engineering had major impacts on the productivity of metal mining in Cornwall. Coupled with increasing demand for tin, copper and lead from across the British Empire, Cornish mining boomed and with it the economy.

At the beginning of the Industrial Revolution, Crantock was a village based on small scale farms. Newquay (Towan Blystra) was virtually undeveloped, certainly there was no usable harbour until the middle of the 19th Century. However, as the technology started to evolve, nearby neighbourhoods began to develop their mines. Between Newlyn East and Rejerrah there were mines for most metals. Old Shepherds mine, proved very productive between 1750 and 1800. This was followed in the early 1800's by the development of lead mining at Wheal Rose. It was these early mines that established the foundation for much of the wealth of the Trewithen Estate. East Wheal Rose soon followed with over 20 shafts and one of the biggest steam engines ever installed in Cornwall, a 100" diameter piston; "The Great Hundred". This engine had been built thirty years before by Harvey's of Hayle for Wheal Vor at Breage. It proved too costly for this tin mine, it consumed around six hundred tons of coal per month, and was decommissioned.

East Wheal Rose operated between 1836 and the late 1880's and was the biggest producer of lead in the UK. It also produced around 6 tonnes of silver during its life. Silver ore usually occurs in conjunction with lead ores. In July 1846 there was a major accident at the mine when a cloud-burst causing the river Gannel to over-flow into the main shaft. 39 miners were drowned and the river was badly silted-up down-stream. In fact, the mine had been discharging pumped water from the beginning, causing the river to silt-up. Settling tanks were eventually built above Trevemper bridge and there were several clear-up operations (manually digging out the silt) to recover the river to allow barges to reach the docks at Trevemper.

As recently as 2016, a survey of the sediments in the river Gannel from Penpol downstream to the sea, discovered significant evidence of lead and zinc contamination. There was a more detailed study in 2000 by Camborne School of Mines between Trenance and Penpol that found very high levels of these metals in core samples taken in the tidal saltings. This latter review considered previous analyses conducted in 1980, that recognised that the Gannel Estuary had the highest lead contamination of any estuary in the south-west. The 2000 study included a sample from just below the bridge at Trenance that: *"reveals the most spectacular down core geochemical variation observed. The extreme enrichment in Lead (in excess of 8500 ppm), Zinc (in excess of 1600 ppm), Rare Earth Elements (Th, Y, Ce, La, and Nd) and Silver."*

Whilst the Newlyn Downs mines were the biggest in the area, there were smaller lead mines in Newquay, many of which date back to the mid-18th Century. These were situated on the banks of the Gannel at Chiverton Wheal Rose, Trethellan, Lehenver, Mount Wise (this mine was used as Newquay's water supply in the late 1800's) and Newquay Consuls in the area of the golf course. There was also a mine, Crantock Consuls, near Trerew farm. All of these mines were relatively small although the Trethellan mine did boast a 60" steam engine in 1863.

There are also records of small lead and silver mines dotted around the region from Cubert to Penhale and Ellenglaze. There is even anecdotal evidence that there may have been some mining activity in Vosporth hill and Trevowah road.

In addition to the lead mines, a very large lode of iron ore was discovered to the west of Penhale, running from Gravel Hill at the north end of Perran sands, inland through Mount and Treamble towards Rejerrah – the Great Perran Iron Lode. The iron was mined by shafts and open cast from the 1840's to the early twentieth century and produced around 200,000 tonnes of ore together with copper, lead and zinc.

With all this mining activity, there was a need for a port from which to ship the ores to smelters in South Wales and to import coal for the steam engines. The Gannel was a recognised port and it is probable that lead ore had been shipped from the river when the earliest Newlyn and Newquay mines were working in the 18th century. The smelting industry in South Wales had grown around the abundant supply of coal. A Cornish family, the Vivians from St Columb, recognised the business opportunity of opening a copper smelting facility in South Wales. John Henry Vivian had started working for a Welsh business and in 1810 he established his own facility at Harford near Swansea. This became a highly profitable operation and financed the building of the Vivian's house at Singleton Manor. The business passed from father to his sons, Henry, Arthur and Richard who continued its development, diversifying into other metals and the production of chemicals such as sulphuric acid. Whilst it had been built on importing copper ore from the South-West, it rapidly expanded to import ore from across the world; from South America to Australia. By 1840, the copper smelting facility was the largest in the world, treating around 40% of the total copper production. The Vivian family financed much of the development of Swansea and they continued to have close connections with the business until 1924. After this, it went through several multi-national owners, including ICI, before finally closing in 1980.

It is clear that some of the lead ore was either smelted at Newlyn East or at the smelting works opposite Fernpit on the banks of the Gannel. There is a crude chamber cut into the rock opposite Fernpit that is almost certainly an early smelting pit suggesting that lead was smelted in this area from a very early date. The Tithe map of 1839 shows a smelting house built on the level ground above the rocks opposite Fernpit with a flue extending up the side of the valley to a chimney stack in the field. The base of the chimney can still be traced in the field leading to the caravan park. The smelter, was a retired army man (Royal Artillery), John Stewart, who, according to the tithe records, lived in the Round House.

It was not only lead that was being smelted in Crantock because an auction notice in 1830 includes a "new built" silver smelting and dwelling house. There is no clear evidence where this facility was although it is possible that it was near the Round House. Silver often occurs alongside lead and there were a number of mines in the area that were listed as lead and silver mines. These

included the Newlyn Downs mines as well as Wheal Golden, Penhale, that operated around 1825, and Wheal Beer (same time and listed as being in Crantock but probably Cubert). There is a village story that a solid plate of silver was lodging in the Old Albion before shipment to London.

Until Joseph Treffry developed the harbour at Newquay, in the middle of the nineteenth century, and constructed the horse drawn tramways to his port, the Gannel was a significant shipping centre although vessels could not go much further inland than the Fernpit. Crantock was listed as a Cornish port in the 13th century and there is evidence that it was navigable as far as Trevemper bridge until mine working further up-stream caused major silting. Trevemper had substantial quays, even in the early 19th century, when it was owned by a member of the Martyn family who also owned Penpol, Tregunnel and Trevithick. In 1949, the Western Morning News published an article describing the details within a set of ledgers that had been discovered. These described the financial dealings of the Martyn family's Trevemper business between 1793 and 1850. Sadly, the whereabouts of these ledgers is not known, despite searches amongst the current Martyn archives held in Kresen Kernow. The ledger contained some intriguing examples of the cost of living during the time. In 1805, a new barge (35' long by 12' 3"), was bought for £52 10s, although this did insist that wood was used from the existing vessel. In 1804, eight barge loads of sand for Thomas Prater (who farmed at Trevemper) cost 14s. The ledger also shows that after the East Wheal Rose mine disaster, the bridge was swept away and huge quantities of silt were deposited in the river so that barges could only be brought to Trevemper on spring tides. "Spading the marsh", at £3 3s to remove silt appeared to be a regular activity.

Iron ore was transported by horse and cart from the Perran mines to holding areas alongside Beach Road. It would be interesting to trace the line of the early horse-drawn wagon track from the mines to Crantock. Lead ore was carried by wagons from Newlyn Downs as far as Trevemper for loading into the barges. These would then carry the ore down-river to the Fernpit. On at least one occasion, the bargees were unable to hold the barge against the rapidly ebbing tide at the Fernpit. While one jumped ashore, the other was swept out to sea on the barge and was eventually rescued off Carters (Gull) rocks, Holywell!

Lead ore would either be smelted at the Crantock works or, be loaded at the Fernpit onto small sailing ships, 100 - 200 tons, that would often take their cargo to Padstow, although some would sail directly to South Wales. All of the iron ore was smelted in Wales. Many of the small ships are recorded in newspaper "Shipping Notices", and they included the *Breeze* (under the master Billing), *Tamar*, *Mary and Elizabeth*, *Charlotte* and many more.

Padstow was a significant port with sailings to all parts of Britain, Europe and even America. It acted as a staging post for the mining industry with small ships bringing their cargoes of ore for transfer to larger ships that sailed onwards to South Wales. These ships would then return to Padstow with coal that would be transferred to the smaller ships to be taken to places like Porth beach, Crantock, Trevaunance and so on. The only record of a much bigger ship coming into the Gannel was in 1858 when the first steam powered, iron built ship, the Kilarney of 500 tons called to collect a cargo of iron ore bound for South Wales.

Cornwall is almost unique in being surrounded by the sea. This encouraged the use of sea-transport rather than roads so that the road system in Cornwall was under-developed until late in the 19th and early 20th century. Small sailing ships would be constantly operating between ports like the Gannel bringing supplies, in addition to coal and ore, such as building materials and lime for fertilizer. Unfortunately, the sea-passage from south to north coast involved the hazardous Land's End waters and it was partly for this reason that Joseph Treffry invested so heavily in creating the tramway network and developing the harbours at Newquay and Par.

The need for small ships encouraged local carpenters to start building ships and between 1820's and 1870's three generations of the Clemens family established a thriving business at Tregunnel. The majority of their ships were between 100 and 200 tons, one or two-masted schooners, that were built on the side of the river. However, from the Martyn ledger it is known that there was ship-building along the Gannel from much earlier.

Once the harbour had opened in Newquay, horse-drawn tramways were constructed from the major mining areas. East Wheal Rose was connected by 1849 and the Perran mines were connected over the next 20 years. Around 1862 a railway was constructed from Newquay to Newlyn Downs and later to Goohavern and Perranporth with a spur from Shepherds down through Treamble to service the iron mines. This track eventually also served as access into the Penhale military establishment during the 2nd World War. Once rail connections had been established, the importance of the Gannel as a shipping centre diminished from around 1850 although ship-building continued until the end of the century. In 1904, a major geological survey of the Newquay area stated that the river Gannel was completely silted and that no shipping now entered the refuge.

Looking at the changing pattern of work, there are no reliable census figures until 1841 that record personal details of people living in the parish. There is no clear picture of how the occupations of the inhabitants of Crantock changed over the busiest period of the Gannel shipping before 1840. However, from 1841 to the end of the century, it is evident from the censuses that there were miners and associated craftspeople living in the village. The 1841 census records that Richard George was the publican of the Miners Inn at Halwyn (now Wayside). In both 1851 and 1861 there were 10 miners, many listed as lodgers, and split between lead and iron mining. These people would have had to walk to work, either in Newlyn East or Penhale. There was even an engine driver (S.T Machine?) living in the village in 1881.

By 1891 they had all disappeared and Crantock was returning to being almost entirely a farming based community. Indeed, the Cornish mining industry had started to decline from the middle of the nineteenth century as overseas mines, with cheap labour and often shallow workings could undercut the prices of the deep mines for Cornwall. Many of these overseas mines were funded by British investors and managed by people who had been educated and trained at the mining schools in Cornwall. Questions were raised in Parliament about the ethics of British investors financing these overseas businesses that were effectively damaging the national industry.

The principal landowner, by a long way, during the period of the Industrial Revolution was the Hawkins family of the Trewithen estate. The 1st Baronet, who never married, lived his entire life in Cornwall between 1758 and his death in 1829. His life covered the first half of the Industrial Revolution and he made great benefit from it. He had inherited much of his land from his father, Thomas, but he dedicated his life to expanding the estate, primarily through exploiting mining and engineering in Cornwall. Between 1798 and 1840 he purchased most, if not all, of the Bishop of Exeter's land in Crantock.

As an aside, Christopher's father Thomas, who had a morbid fear of catching smallpox, died after having an inoculation to prevent it. Two of his brothers also died in unusual circumstances; an older brother drowned while at Eton and a younger brother died of a fever as a consequence of "eating ice-cream after dancing".

The 1st Baronet claimed that he could "ride from one side of Cornwall to the other without setting hoof on another man's soil." He was the Lord Lieutenant of Cornwall and the Vice Lord Warden of the Stannaries. This position gave him significant influence over the mining businesses in Cornwall. He owned mines at Newlyn East (Lead), St Ives (Copper & Tin), Ladock (gold), St Austell (China Clay) and was a partner in the Cornish Copper company that built the Copperhouse smelting works in Hayle. He also developed the harbours at Hayle, St Ives and Pentewan. He was a patron of Richard Trevithick and, 1812, he commissioned the first portable steam threshing machine that was working until 1880 and is now preserved in the Science Museum.

The 1st Baronet invested very significantly in developing the gardens at Trewithen, much of which survives to this day. On top of all this he was also a Member of Parliament, associated with the Rotten Boroughs of Grampound, Mitchell and Penryn. In this latter ward he was found guilty of bribery and lost his seat. He was also a renowned miser of whom it was said:

"*A large house, and no cheer,*
A large park, and no deer,
A large cellar, and no beer,
Sir Christopher Hawkins lives here."

Following the death of the 1st Baronet, in 1829, the estate passed to his younger brother, John, who was an eminent geologist and horticulturalist. John was a Fellow of the Royal Society, a founding member of the Royal Horticultural Society and Royal Geological Society of Cornwall, as well as an honorary member of the Geological Society of London. He died in 1841 and the estate passed to his son, another Christopher Henry Hawkins who appears to have never set foot in Cornwall. The Trewithen estate continues to this day.

Another major landowner was the Boscawen (Lord Falmouth) family from the Tregothnan. At the start of the Industrial Revolution, the estate was managed by Hugh Boscawen, the 1st Viscount. Hugh made a fortune from his mining interests around Gwennap and Chacewater. In the mid-1700's this area of land, around Wheal Busy, was known as the "richest square mile on earth". It was one of the first mining areas to install steam pumping engines. Wheal Busy produced over 100,000 tons of copper ore, and 27,000 tons of arsenic that contributed much to the wealth of the Boscawen family. Hugh owned Treago manor and other parcels of land within the parish. In 1734, the estate passed to his son, another Hugh, who was a successful army officer and politician. He died in 1782 with no legitimate children (he had 3 illegitimate children) and the estate passed to his nephew, George, who was also a politician and army officer. When George died in 1808, the estate passed to his son, Edward who remained head of the family until 1841 when his son, another George, took over. He died in 1852 and he was succeeded by his cousin, Evelyn Boscawen who lived until 1889. Evelyn was a very successful racehorse owner and won many English classics including the Derby (twice), 1000gns, 2000gns, Oaks and St Leger. The Falmouth stakes run at Newmarket every July is in memory of Evelyn Boscawen.

It is not clear how prosperous the Boscawen family was during the 19th century as they appear to have reduced their landowning in Crantock quite substantially between 1800 and the 1840 tithe census. Treago had been sold on to the Hawke family and there had been an auction of the Old Albion in 1840 together with a couple of small parcels of land, including the area where Hevlas now stands, as a result of a writ issued by the Vice-Warden of the Stannaries of Cornwall (was this Sir

Christopher Hawkins, and if so was there any love lost between these families?)

Of other landowning families at the beginning of the 19th century, the tithe holder, the Buller family appears to have only retained a small area of land by the 1840's. Similarly, all the other titled owners had disappeared. However, the yeomen families, Hosken, Stephens, Johns and Martyn, had substantially increased their holdings. Of the new landowners, one of the more unusual names is Ezekiel Gavid (or Gaved).

Gavid was a farmer from Tregennow, St Mewan, outside St Austell. His family bought this farm at auction in 1801 but his father, Captain James Gavid (94) and his mother (70) died together in May 1821. His father could have been either a retired mine captain or a ships' captain. A couple of years before their deaths, Ezekiel Gavid was in court giving evidence against John Pappin who was charged with stealing one of the Gavid's sheep. The poor man was found guilty and hanged at Bodmin jail.

There is no obvious connection between the Gavid family and Crantock apart from Ezekiel owning a number of fields scattered randomly around the outskirts of the village. The family appears to have remained based in the St Austell area and in 1866 they sold all of their Crantock land-holdings in five Lots. This probably coincides with the death of Ezekiel as he was 82 in the 1861 census. William Martyn was listed as the tenant at the time of the auction, and it seems likely that he purchased the free-hold of the land. There is a receipt in the Martyn archive, for Lot 1 for £1100 from John Gavid (assumed to be Ezekiel's heir) to William Martyn dated 9 Oct 1866. Lot 1 included the Ship Inn and several buildings in the centre of the village. It is assumed that William also bought the other 4 Lots in the sale. Indeed, William's will specifically identifies all the properties bought from the Gavid family in 1866 and describes them collectively as the Gaved Tenement. One of the plots of land, Mitchell's Sandy Close, is where my house is. My father purchased the land from Miss Martyn of Boskenna in 1955.

A letter to the Royal Cornwall Gazette of July 1898 sums up Crantock at the end of the 19th century Industrial Revolution,

Sir, as a visitor to Crantock I would thank you to insert the following in the columns of your valuable paper, knowing you are ever ready and willing to assist in bringing about a healthy state of things:

1. *The well in the village is a pit….. The water in it had a bad and offensive smell. Often, after rain it is the colour of mud, as water from the road and farmyards wash into it.. It is little more than a catch-pit*
2. *Drains from the pig-houses, and slops from some of the houses, are thrown into a cess-pit not more than five feet from the front door.*

3. Houses within the village are without w.c.s
4. Another well, or shoot, in the lower part of the village runs parallel with the road with dung-heaps and a cess-pit over and beside it.
5. A thick layer of deposits from many geese covers the ground of the village.

On making inquiry, I found members of the County Council had been here some few weeks ago, and had condemned most of these nuisances, but nothing has been done.
The sanitary inspector, I find, lives at St Columb Major. Should he come to Crantock I should find great pleasure in proving all I have stated in this letter.
Signed H D Hawke

CHAPTER 7

A Divided Society

On 28 February 1865, Salathiel Sleeman was charged at the St Columb Petty Sessions with the indecent assault of Elizabeth Rickeard on 1 February. The basis for the charge was that Salathiel had called at Anthony Mitchell's farm to inquire about a threshing machine. Anthony was visiting Truro and Elizabeth, who worked as Anthony's servant, was alone. She admitted that she had invited Salathiel in for a glass of cider but she claimed, that after they had finished drinking, he assaulted her. She claimed that she had managed to escape, tearing her dress, that was presented as evidence, in the process. Salathiel asserted that she had been a consenting partner. The bench decided that there was a case to answer and it was referred to the next assize in Bodmin. However, no bail conditions were imposed. It seems that there was considerable interest in the case and a significant crowd of people assembled outside the court.

1865 was the year in which the American civil war came to an end in April when Robert E Lee surrendered, although it did rumble on into the summer. This was quickly followed, literally a few days later, by the assassination of President Abraham Lincoln at Ford's theatre in Washington.

The Cornish mining industry was still significant although Crantock's importance as an export facility for lead and iron ore had declined as the harbour at Newquay developed. Even so, in 1861, there were still 8 or 9 lead and iron miners living in the village although the majority were engaged in farming. However, the great mining days of the nineteenth century were over and ten years later, in 1875, over 10,000 miners left Cornwall to work overseas, including South Australia where over 40% of the new arrivals were from Cornwall. And remember that South Australia was colonized by emigrants, no convicts were deported to this region! Within 10 years, South Australian mines would overtake Cornwall as the biggest producer of copper in the British Empire. Even today, over 10% of South Australians can trace their ancestry back to Cornwall and they host the biggest Cornish festival in the world, Kernewek Lowender that attracts over 35,000 people biannually.

The story of Salathiel Sleeman is centred on three Crantock farms: Trew (now Trerew), Treworthal and Trewolla that are all within a few miles of each other, straddling the Goonhavern to Newquay road (A3075). In 1865 all of these farms were in the parish of Crantock and were owned by the Trewithen Estate of Sir Christopher Hawkins, who could proudly boast that he could ride from the South to North coasts without setting foot in anybody else's land. He had made a considerable fortune through ownership of tin, lead and copper mines.

At the time of the incident, in 1865, Salathiel lived with his mother Susan as tenants at Trew farm. He was 28 and a bachelor. Salathiel's father Arthur had been killed seven years before (at the age of 58) in an accident in which the horse that he was driving had bolted and Arthur was thrown from the wagon. At 200 acres, Trew farm was large by standards at that time.

Salathiel had two brothers, Jonathon (two years his elder) and Zacheus (21) and he had two sisters; Catherine (26) and Selina (13). Zacheus would eventually take over Trew farm from his mother and we will hear more of him later.

The next major character in this story is Anthony Mitchell who was married to Ulelya (who came from St Columb Minor). He farmed Trewolla that was just to the west of Trew Farm. His father, also called Anthony, had farmed Trewolla before him but he now lived in Cubert and sadly he died in the next year at the age of 84. Young Anthony married Ulelya nine years before this story, and the 1861 and 1871 censuses list his wife as a resident at the farm. However, during 1865, Anthony claims that he was not living with his wife. As you will see, there may be more to Anthony Mitchell than meets the eye. At the time of this story, Anthony had a housekeeper, Elizabeth Rickeard. The other characters in this story, are principally servants who worked for these and other yeomen farmers.

After his appearance at the Petty Sessions, Salathiel's case was eventually heard in March at Bodmin assizes, where he was defended by a QC, Mr Karslake and a solicitor Mr Bullen. It is interesting that the defendant was clearly able to summon considerable legal expertise for his defence. After presentation of the case, the jury retired for over two hours before they returned a verdict of "not guilty". There was much rejoicing at the verdict and Salathiel was borne away to the Town Arms to "*lusty cheering*"! This story illustrates the division in the society of that time between the yeomen and their workers.

In the year that Salathiel was charged, indeed just a month after his acquittal, he was robbed of a horse and its tack. The following day, the thief did a deal with Harry Cottle in St Tudy, selling the horse for £7.50 and taking a pony in part-exchange. The next day, he was riding the pony when he met John Hosken who was driving his Jersey cow to Bodmin fair. He exchanged the pony and tack plus 50p for the cow that he apparently then took to Bodmin. Unfortunately, he was known there and arrested by Inspector Woods who recognized that he had been given three years for sheep-stealing and was currently on "ticket-of-leave" (parole). The thief was called John Manuel (47) and he was sent from Camelford magistrates to Bodmin Assizes where he was tried in June. He was found guilty and, because he had several previous convictions, he was sentenced to 7 years penal servitude.

The term penal servitude resulted from the Penal Servitude act of 1853 and it meant a term of imprisonment with hard labour. The Act replaced the transportation of convicted criminals to Australia with detention in "convict prisons" in the UK. The Act also introduced the facility for early release of prisoners on "conditional licence" or "ticket-of-leave".

In 1866, a year after the alleged sexual assault, Salathiel married Eliza Roberts from St Columb, so clearly the incident with Elizabeth Rickeard had been forgiven! Salathiel and Eliza went on to have 2 children by the time of the 1871 census, Henry (4) and Little Eliza (1). Salathiel had also taken over the 130 acre Treworthal farm (along the road from the Plains).

By 1871, Salathiel employed two General Servants, Mary Roberts (30) and Mary Rickard (11) who were both born in St Newlyn East and two Field Servants, Samuel Benney (21, born in Mawgan) and John Rowland who was only 12 and was born in Plymouth. From the records of this period it is apparent that there were many inter-family relations between the three principal parishes of Crantock, St Columb Minor and St Newlyn East.

Anthony Mitchell and Salathiel Sleeman both were serving as churchwardens of Crantock church in 1867 and they were present at the Annual Vestry at the Albion

Inn that was chaired by Mr W Martyn of Penpol in March 1867.

Clearly, Salathiel was seen as an upstanding character in the parish, which would account for the large crowds that attended both the Petty Session and Assizes for the charge of indecent assault in 1865.

Incidentally, Salathiel sold up in 1880 and retired from farming. He is buried in Crantock church-yard beside the Prater family graves (inside the gate and to the right).

Anthony Mitchell has an intriguing set of side stories, that may explain why he was separated from his wife at the time of the assault!

Three years after the "Salathiel's incident", in 1868, Anthony Mitchell was in court accusing Sarah Jane Coad Powell of stealing his bag containing between £10 and £12. The accused had previously been his housekeeper. The episode happened in Truro when the accused had met Mitchell and *"a few words passed between them"*! Later, when Mitchell was driving home with his horse and cart he passed the accused walking up Kenwyn Hill and she asked for a ride. He agreed but after a short-time felt his coat being tugged and the accused had his handkerchief in her hand. He stopped and put the accused off his wagon before driving on. It was then that he realized that his bag and money were gone. So, he drove back and caught up with the accused whom he challenged and asked a passer-by to go back to Truro and fetch the police. His bag was retrieved from the hedge and Sarah Jane was arrested.

At the trial, Sarah pleaded that she had taken the money but that she was not guilty of stealing it. The magistrate told her she had to plead either guilty or not guilty without any form of qualification and if not guilty then she would be committed for trial at the assizes. She, pleaded guilty but stated her case that she had borne an illegitimate son by Mitchell and that she had sought maintenance through the courts but she could not raise enough money to pay for a witness to travel from Truro and her mother had also died just before the court session. She claimed that Mitchell had written to her and asked her to come to a meeting to discuss the maintenance. There appeared to have been several such meetings and the accused also claimed that they met in Truro on the day of the incident by prior agreement. He had claimed that he was *"so poor as death"* and offered her 1s 2d (about 11p) that she had refused. She then claimed that he had told her to look in his pockets and it was there that she found the bag that she was accused of stealing. It also transpired that after arrest, the police had a collection to pay for her bed for the night!

Despite the poor woman having no previous problems, the magistrate found her guilty and sentenced her to 14 days in the County goal. No doubt, if the magistrate had not had some sympathy for her story it could have been a very much stricter sentence. Her version of events seems highly likely bearing in mind some of the other shenanigans that Anthony Mitchell was involved in, for Anthony's story continues! On the one-hand we have an upstanding member of the local community, Churchwarden, Vestry and Schoolboard member (Just looking at the names of the original board is a roll call of old Crantock names: Chegwidden, Stephens, Martyn, Rowe, Morcomb, Johns and Sleeman), charity dispenser (in 1870, he organised a parish collection to provide food for the poor at Christmas), member of the Cornwall County Chamber of Agriculture, agent for a shipping company and recognised authority on sheep. On the other had we find that in June 1873 he was fined £2 for assaulting John Andrew at the St Columb Fair. In 1874 he was involved in a case over the sale of a horse and, one year later, in May, he was again fined, £1, for the *"brutal assault"* of Mary Ann Taylor. Mary claimed that she had borne two illegitimate children by Anthony. Not content with that, he was later charged with *"furious driving"* in July and, in 1877 he was again fined, this time for driving a threshing machine without reins and, finally, in 1878, he was fined 25p for *"pulling out the whiskers"* of J Hendy from Mawgan.

Anthony Mitchell died in 1880, at the young age of 54, and there were glowing tributes in the local press. It is likely that he died from typhoid as there was a major outbreak of the disease in Newlyn East at this time. His wife, Ulelya, appears to have returned and she continued to farm Trewolla for the next twenty years into the 1900's. They had no children but he does seem to have left several descendants behind amongst his servants!

The Sleeman family also has an intriguing story attached to it. Salathiel's younger brother Zaccheus, he was seven year's younger than Salathiel, lived with his mother at Trew farm until, in December 1866, he married Jemima Hicks, the daughter of a blacksmith from Newquay. It appears that Zaccheus and Jemima took over Trew farm and his mother moved to Treworthal with his brother Salathiel and his family. In 1871, the census lists Zaccheus and Jemima living at Trew with their two children, Susan (3) and John (2). However, newspapers also report that all of the livestock and machinery was sold off in September, *"in consequence of the family leaving at Michaelmas"*. Presumably, this was the end of their tenancy agreement with the Trewithen estate.

Purely by chance, Zaccaheus crops up again, five years later, in 1876, when he arrives in New Zealand on board the Merwanjee Framjee! What a trip he must have had because the time for the passage was one of the quickest ever recorded, less than seventy-seven days. This was almost three weeks faster than expected and her time from Gravesend to the equator, seventeen days, was only equalled by the famous Cutty Sark. The master of the ship, Captain Bidwell, seems quite a character because he hove-too in the south Atlantic to *"have a tot"* with the Captain of a passing Yankee ship, the

Chatanooga. The Merwanjee Framjee was a three-masted, 1079 ton, clipper ship built by John Reid, Glasgow in 1863. On this trip, she carried twelve steerage passengers to Auckland before returning via Port Adelaide to load a cargo of wheat for Liverpool.

The Merwanjee Framjee had a long and distinguished life being employed on many of the long sea passages around the globe from UK to Australia, New Zealand, South America, Canada and the United States. She finally met her end in 1906 when she was wrecked on Red Island, Newfoundland while on voyage from Quebec to Buenos Aires.

Records show that Zaccaheus's wife, Jemima, and their children remained in the Crantock area. Whatever precipitated his sudden departure to New Zealand is unknown but sadly he never came home and he died in New Zealand in October 1885 after *"fitting"*. He had spent the last years of his life working as a farm-hand in Waikato for a man called Jenkins, almost certainly another Cornish emigrant.

Salathiel too eventually gave up farming at Treworthal in 1880 although, even when he was retired, he managed to get into trouble in 1888 for being drunk in Pydar street and fined 25p with costs!

So much for Salathiel and Anthony and the Yeoman classes but what of the servant girl Elizabeth Rickeard who brought the charge against Salathiel? While the lives of the Sleeman brothers and Anthony Mitchell have been relatively easy to track, that of Mary Rickeard, the servant girl who started this story, has been more difficult to trace. Indeed, whilst the lives of the upper-class and yeomen (middle) class members of the nineteenth century can be pieced together relatively easily from parish records and newspaper reports, the working classes are much more difficult.

Elizabeth was probably the daughter of Richard Rickard (57), a farmer from Quintrel Downs who is listed in the 1861 census as owning a farm of just 15 acres. Richard was married to Mary (55) and they had three children living with them, William (24), Elizabeth (20) and Israel (13). They also had two grandchildren Susan (17) and Herbert (1m), although it is unclear whether these belonged to the "live-in" children. However, it seems reasonable to suppose that life for such a large family living off a small farm would have been difficult and therefore it does seem highly likely that Elizabeth would be sent away to work.

The Sleeman family also figure in another episode involving a servant girl. Brother Zacheus Sleeman was involved in a case just two years after our story of 1865, when one of his servants, Mary Jane May, stole a half a sovereign from another servant. She was arrested by PC Pearce from Newlyn East who established that she had bought a dress with the money from a local shop. She was committed to trial at the magistrates in St Columb and in October 1867, where she was sentenced to four months hard labour.

Her sentence was served in the St Columb Union work-house where she was involved in what the papers described as a *"disgraceful case"* involving a young prisoner, Elizabeth Ann Knight. Elizabeth had given birth to an illegitimate baby in the work-house. The baby had not been well since birth and the conditions in which both mother and baby were kept appear to have been appalling. The baby boy had limited clothing (he was dressed in "union" clothes with nothing on his feet) and there was very little sympathy for both mother and baby.

Eventually, the mother deliberately broke a pane of glass in the work-house, and then refused to work. Mary Jane May was a witness to the incident and she accompanied the policeman and Elizabeth to a magistrate in Padstow. It seems that they walked to Padstow from St Columb. On return, Elizabeth and the baby were imprisoned in the "clink" that was attached to the work-house. She was then given the option of either walking to Bodmin goal or waiting for transport.

She was so desperate to get away from the work-house that she chose to walk with the baby and accompanied by a Constable they set off. It was bitterly cold and the party stopped at the Victoria Inn, Roche, for lunch. Eventually they got to Bodmin but as they were passing the asylum the baby became very distressed and when they arrived at Bodmin Goal the poor thing was found to have died. The Coroner's jury was very critical of the way in which the mother and baby had been treated in the work-house and both the master and matron were blamed for the infant's death. However, it was not recorded whether any action was taken against them.

A sad end to our story but it illustrates how severe life was for the "have-nots" during the nineteenth century. Servants were treated badly by society and sentences for transgressing laws, were draconian. Up until 1853, people were transported for what we would consider minor crimes, such as stealing a coat, and it was not until the Penal Servitude act of 1853 that transportation was effectively stopped. There was also a big divide in the way that justice was dispensed across the classes in society. Men from the middle and upper classes appear to have received favourable treatment compared with women from the working classes.

But before we finish, some more cheerful "clippings" from 1865.

The 150 ton Edith was launched from the Clemens shipyard at Tregunnel for Captain Chegwidden. This 'yard continued to build ships to the end of the century but the Gannel was now in decline.

The main road to Trevemper bridge was in such a poor state of repair that it was impassable for a horse and carriage.

In September, at Mawgan, the local publican waded into the surf and, after an hour-long struggle, hauled a 15' shark ashore. It had been chasing pilchards when it got stranded. Then, a month later (in October!) a lady was swimming at Crantock when her maid saw a shark approaching. Apparently the *"lady, very prudently made a speedy exit from the water"*. The ladies were convinced that it was a white shark and the newspaper concluded that it must have been the mate of the shark captured at Mawgan.

Four ladies of *"questionable character"* living in Crantock were each fined 2s 6d for assaulting a Padstow innkeeper. Two pairs of sisters; Fanny & Mary Scoble and Jane and Elizabeth Morrish.

Finally, Jane Davis from Perranzabuloe was sent to prison for 14 days for stealing a shovel belonging to Peter Tozer (aged 42), a highway labourer from Trevemper and father of 9 children ranging from 18 to 3 months!

CHAPTER 8

Bohemian Crantock

If we begin in the 1920s, we have a county recovering from the Great War and a time when Cornwall's mining industry had declined considerably. Although even as late as 1919, there were still a few profitable mines and in October of that year, the top linkage of the man-engine at the Levant mine sheared and 32 men were killed as it collapsed down the shaft. Crantock, together with every village in the Cornwall, contributed to the Lord Lieutenant's fund for the relatives. Crantock contributed £9-16s-9p (compared with Cubert 13gns!). The disappearance of mining connections to Crantock were noted in an obituary in 1922 for Charlotte Harris who died in Crantock at the age of 91. She was something of a local "character" and could remember when the mines were in full swing and *"much drinking was indulged in"*. She would have remembered when the Gannel was thriving with ships importing coal and exporting lead and iron ore. When there was an active lead smelting works on the side of the Gannel (that closed around 1840), opposite Fernpit, ships were being built at Tregunnel and Crantock was a busy "working village" populated mainly by those engaged in farming, mining and the sea. We should also remember that the parish of Crantock included East Pentire and farms to the east (such as Trerew).

The 1920's began to see significant changes to the village. A mineral tramway and later a railway had been constructed into Newquay in the second half of the 19th century and the railway had been taken over by Great Western Railway in 1896 when it was linked to the mainline at Par. The arrival of the railway and expansion of Newquay harbour, coupled with the dramatic silting of the river, virtually killed off the marine trading that had been based in the Gannel through the 18th and 19th centuries.

The GWR began to promote Newquay as a holiday destination because the revenue from transporting ore and china clay had declined significantly as Par docks expanded. However, Crantock remained isolated as the road from Newquay was tortuous and went through Treloggan before descending to Trevemper and thence on to Crantock. It was not until 1926 that the present Gannel road was built that shortened the journey. This was a major development and was accompanied by the building of a new bridge at Trevemper. In 1939, an order was finally approved by Cornwall Quarter sessions at Bodmin, granting Cornwall County Council permission to close the old bridge. The chairman, Col Tangye remarked that the new bridge was "the most hideous bridge I have seen in my life" and recommended that a campaign be started to preserve the old structure.

Three years after the Gannel road was opened, the telephone network was extended from Newquay to

Crantock and West Pentire and in May 1935, new power cables were approved for installation along the same route. Our isolation was coming to an end.

An interesting debate took place before and after the Gannel road was built and this concerned improving the road connection to Crantock via a bridge or dam. There were suggestions of running a road across the river at Trenance and then down the valley to Penpol (this mirrored a much earlier proposal for a railway that would have connected Crantock to the mines at Perran). But in 1931, the Duchy commissioned a study to consider a dam across the river at Penpol that would both support a new road from Tregunnel and a tidal-electric scheme to provide electricity for Newquay. The initial suggestion was for a temporary electric power station to prove the technology. There was considerable support for this proposal and there was much correspondence in the press about it after an application was made to the Board of Trade by consultant engineers (who are now Mott Macdonald) on behalf of a private company (Tidal Energy Ltd) in May for the construction. Tidal Energy Ltd were to fund the experiment that was based on a set of turbines that would work on the ebb and flood of the tide. Energy would be stored in compressed air cylinders to be released through air turbines during "slack tides". This type of renewable energy is now very much back on the agenda! There appears to have been a bitter conflict in the town with people being asked to sign a petition to oppose the plan "or their rates would go up". Hedley

Westlake (an ex town councillor) was very critical of the protestors and their standing in the way of progress!

In the end, it appears to have fizzled out, but not too sure of the reasons.

In the 1920's, the Gannel summer regatta was thriving with the banks lined by thousands of spectators to watch rowing, sailing, motor boat and swimming races, together with shore-line entertainment such as the greasy-pole, Miller & Sweep and fireworks. Strangely, the Gannel regatta faltered occasionally in the '30s and was cancelled in a number of years. There were baby shows (Beatrice Wills came 2nd in the under 3 months in Sept 1920), local agricultural shows, ploughing matches and bell ringing competitions. An Arts & Crafts Fair was held in the Old Forge in June 1925. Almost all of these diversions have now disappeared.

The 1920's and 30's saw an expansion of the number of tourists coming to the village and a clear shift away from the reliance on farming as the major employer in the region. It is obvious from advertisements that several properties in the village were being let for holidays and people were being employed to service them. One example is for a nursemaid for Mrs Grew at Kareena for July 1921 with a view to moving to Denmark at the end of the summer. Does anybody remember the Grew family who stayed in Beach road in the 1950's while on leave from Kowloon? There was also a Mr H B Grew, from Crantock, who was badly injured when a Western National omnibus hit a telegraph pole in Cubert in July 1929. Were they a local family?

In 1930, Nils Soderberg (who was from London but owned property in the village) was bemoaning the development that was taking place to "this charming old world village". The "hideous, drab looking" Council houses at Halwyn and the "Barracks" on West Pentire road, with their corrugated iron garages, were all cited by Soderberg in a letter to the Western Morning News.

Soderberg also pointed out that there were only 3 or 4 artistically attractive bungalows that had been built in the village "but these were not built for any local people". All sounds familiar to the present day!

Interestingly, in 1939, Soderberg (a Swede who changed his name when the second world war broke out) was ordered to pay damages of £11-15s to Edith Rickard for cracking the walls of her house while his contractor Albert Lobb was blasting a well at the adjacent property in West Pentire!

In 1920s, houses like Boskenna (designed by Alwyn Martyn for Isabel Martyn when she moved from Penpol), Sandy Close (the original that is), Vigornia (a tiny beach bungalow before it was overwhelmed by modernization) and Lewannoc (the original, it has burned down twice in my life-time) were built. Would any of these have been allowed under today's planning rules?

Sandy Close was built for a Miss Wheeler in the early 1930s and she was advertising for a cook in July 1937 to cater for 8 people and 4 staff. She was a share-holder in Crittal's galvanized windows who supplied "double-dipped" frames for the windows of Sandy Close. Many were quite grand houses and it would appear that they were often built as summer retreats for the wealthy people from Cornwall and also from Oxford, London and Birmingham.

One of the more unusual residences was the schooner Ada that was moored in Penpol. She was old, built in 1876 at Ulverston, and originally registered in Barrow. She was 2 masted, around 133 tons and registered with Lloyd's. She was involved with taking coal around the coast of UK and ended up in the Gannel at the beginning of the twentieth century. The Ada was auctioned in September 1932, complete with a collection of curios, electric light and steam heating. She appears to have been re-sold in 1936/7 to Horatio Hodges Thatcher who ran it as a museum and used to show US soldiers who were billeted in Penpol around his collection. The Ada was sold again to Charlie Force (now there's a subject for a story!) in around 1958 and eventually burned (after the useable timber had been removed). She was replaced with a WW2 MTB. Horatio Thatcher died in St Agnes in 1963.

A more macabre indication of growing tourism is to study the number of reported drownings on the beach! In the 1930's we were averaging nearly one/year with people from London, the North and Midlands.

Aug 1923, Walter Clark, an overseas commercial traveler.
July 1930, Arthur Jones (52) from Warwickshire who worked for the iron and steel tube manufacturer Stewards and Lloyds (note possible link to James Accles).
Aug 1930, John Baker London solicitor
July 1933, Lewis Lockwood a north country man staying at Trevemper
Aug 1935, William Punchard (20) His brother was saved. They had hiring a rowing boat from the ferryman Joseph Morris and warned not to go further than Fernpit because the tide was ebbing. They ignored warnings from boatmen and capsizing at Point Noe. Mr Northey was involved in the rescue of the brother.
Aug 1937, William Matthews from Birmingham drowned saving his father.

But even locals could get into difficulties and drown:

Aug 1929, James Collins (17) and Albert Richards (22) from Penpol and Trevella respectively. Two farm hands who had gone for a swim after harvest.

But now, to consider some of the more "interesting" characters associated with the village.

First, two men who had made major contributions to Crantock Church died at the beginning of the 1920's. The Rev George Metford Parsons who had been instrumental in the renovation (raising over £10,000) died in 1924 and the architect Edmund Sedding predeceased him and was buried in the churchyard in 1921. There are several treaties about these tow influential men. Interestingly, Metford Parsons had an artistic brother, Arthur Worth Parsons, who painted many views of the village and coastline between 1900 and 1920 *(he died in 1931) - Crantock Cornwall, Rocky beach* (1903); *Rocky Foreshore*; *Three Masted Sailing Vessels before the harbour and town of Penzance; Back of the Post Office, Crantock* (1920); *The Old Fish Cellars, Newquay* (1920). He co-founded the Bristol Savages art group with Ernest Ehlers in 1904. The Group visited Cornwall and painted a number of views along the North coast

From the world of engineering there is James Accles who died in Sept 1939. He lived at the Beacon and had a very interesting career. He was born in Bendigo, Australia, in 1850 to Irish parents (this coincided with a gold rush in the area that attracted many Chinese), he was apprentice at Colt Firearms in Connecticut and came to England in 1872. He started a factory making *"caps" for the .42 Russian "Berdan"* cartridges. In 1873 he went to China for the US Gatling Gun Co. and established factories in Canton and Shanghai. Between 1875 and 1886 he opened 15 manufacturing facilities for Gatling

Gun around the world. In 1889 he was appointed engineer-in-charge of the new Gatling Gun Co factory at Holdford Mill, Cheshire but the company went into liquidation a year later. Undaunted, he went into the production of metal tubing and, with his brother, established the Accles motorcycle company. This too failed in 1898 but he re-emerged as Accles & Pollock in 1901 and then after yet more failures, Accles & Shelvoke was formed in 1913 in Birmingham. This company was a big success and manufactured a humane animal stun gun that was promoted by and financed by Christopher Cash (of Cash tape fame) that became a best seller around the world. The company still operates today and is a world market leader making humane stunning equipment and the patented Akvoke cable spiker – a mandated means of testing whether HV cables are live!

Still with engineering, we have Madeline Footner, who lived at Perch Close. Her father had been the Chief Engineer of the London and North West Railway. Madeline subsequently ran a small guest-house at West Pentire. There was also Roland Gouk who lived at the White House in the 1950's who had been an engineer with the Metal Box company. He developed one of the first automated production lines to make boxes. He died in 1962.

There are three particularly interesting artistic families associated with Crantock during this period: The Praters, Nettleships and Johns.

First, and briefly, the Praters who were very much a "Crantock" family with connections going back to the 1700s. The most famous was the artist William whose father, Joseph, had moved away from Crantock to find work in London, probably in the late 1830's. He is not mentioned in the Crantock Census of 1841, although his father, yet another Joseph, and step-mother Ann together with his brother Simon are listed as residents at Halwyn. Joseph was a cordwainer – maker of leather goods such as shoes. While in London, he met and married a Londoner, Jane Harkin, and they produced 9 children over a 20 year period, starting with William in 1851.

The majority of their children do not appear to have married and there were at least three artists. William, worked on the London Illustrated News, Henry was a wood engraver and finally Joseph junior (that makes 3 generations of Josephs and there is another to come!).

Although many of the children remained in London, at least two came back to Halwyn; William in the 1910's and his brother Francis who married Julia Stephens, the daughter of the miller at Treago. Francis & Julia had two sons; Francis (who went back to the London family and worked as a joiner) and Joseph Henry who stayed locally, he studied at Seale Hayne and eventually married and purchased land on West Pentire. A newspaper report in February 1920 states that J.H Prater bought 3 fields, 6 enclosures of 14 acres with a dwelling for £700. Joseph Henry built the West Pentire Hotel in around 1935 (the suggestion is that he deliberately built it to block the view of his brother who lived in the Manor House). In 1945, a travel writer described the hotel as looking like a "barracks or a County Police Station", even though he did give it a good "write-up". Joseph Henry sold the hotel in 1945 to Mrs Monro who renamed it the Crantock Bay Hotel and she eventually sold it to David Eyles father in 1952. Joseph Henry Prater appears to have finally sold his interests in West Pentire in November 1949. A house that he owned (and possibly had built), Talland, was sold the following year, 1950 (when the rates were a mere £10 12s 8d!).

But back to his uncle William who retired from the London Illustrated News and retired to the village and started to paint full-time. Unfortunately, he was only an active artist for 6 years between 1917 and 1923; dying in 1925. William also seems to have been a bit of a letter writer and had several letters published in the Western Morning News. He was particularly vocal against Lady Astor who was championing a bill to prohibit the sale of alcohol. *"What is wanted by the man in the street is better beer and his own time to drink it in!"*

It is William's artist brother Joseph who is credited with carving the lady's head and poem in the Pipers Hole cave. There is some confusion over the several Josephs and Francises and, indeed there was the brother Henry/Harry who exhibited a wood engraving "On the Gannel" in the 1923 Royal Academy exhibition! The carved head is an intriguing piece and it does look as if the carver took trouble to catch somebody's likeness. But, who is the lady? And when was it done? The style suggests the 1920's (when Joseph would have been in his 60's). And is there any meaning in the words of the poem? Was it to commemorate a "lost love"?

There is also the carving of a horse below the head and there is a story that the carving commemorates a girl who was horse-riding and got cut off by the tide and drowned in the cave. All a bit dramatic but I'm afraid there is not a shred of evidence to support this! I have trawled through pages of newspapers from that period, but no mention of any such accident in Crantock. And these were the times when they used to relish a good drowning. The horse carving was, apparently, done much later by a local man – James Dyer.

It is the wife of farmer Joseph Henry Prater that provides the connection to the next two families. Mrs Prater ran a tea-room at West Pentire and she was the last person to see Henry John, son of the famous, some would say infamous, artist Augustus John.

Henry John, disappeared while on holiday with his aunt Ethel Nettleship in 1935. Henry was the last son born to Augustus and his wife Ida in 1907. Unfortunately, Ida died immediately after Henry was born and he was primarily brought up by one of his three aunts, Ursula Nettleship, in Petersfield. There were three Nettleship sisters, Ida – the wife of Augustus, Ursula (who was a singer and voice coach) and Ethel (who was a cellist and lace maker). The sisters were born in Kettering, Northampton, and their father, John Trivett Nettleship, although trained as a solicitor, was an accomplished artist and book illustrator. He was on the fringes of the Pre-Raphaelite brotherhood in London where the family moved in the 1860's.

Between 1903 and 1907, Henry's father, Augustus lived in a menage à trois with his wife Ida and mistress Dorothy McNeill (Dorelia), first in Essex and later in Paris. Ida bore five children, of which one, Caspar, was to rise through the ranks of the Royal Navy to become the First Sea Lord in 1960. Augustus, who was a pacifist, virtually disowned his Naval son.

The mistress, Dorelia had four children by Augustus including sons Pyramus and Romilly (who became a poet). In his life, it is believed that Augustus fathered around 100 children by a variety of women from across London society!

Augustus's son Henry had an interesting early life travelling and eventually attended Campion Hall, Oxford, to train as a priest. However, on completing his studies he decided that this was not the life for him so he went back to Chelsea and became a "philosopher". He clearly kept in contact with the Nettleships and he would come to stay in Crantock with his aunt Ethel.

Ethel owned a bungalow at Quarry Field, although it only appears to have been a holiday home and it was here that Henry had come to stay on 13 June 1935. He disappeared on Saturday the 22 June. The alarm was raised when his car was found abandoned on the lane down to Porth Joke and concerns increased when his Irish Terrier was found alone on the cliffs at Kelsey head. His father, Augustus, came down from London to search and boats were hired from Newquay but he was not found over the following days.

In fact it was not until July that his body washed up on Perranporth beach. The inquest, at which Augustus attended, drew no conclusions about how he had met his death, whether from a fall or simply whilst bathing from the rocks. In his summing up, the Coroner said; "The dog probably is the only one that could tell what happened, and, unfortunately he is dumb". Henry is buried in St Columb Minor church-yard.

It appears that the whole John family used to come to visit and stay with Ethel during the summer and there are stories that Augustus used to live in a caravan in Penpol woods where local children would throw stones onto the roof! Many villagers thought he was just too Bohemian and not to be trusted!

Ethel Nettleship was in the news again just a few months after the inquest on Henry when she was caught driving his car without insurance and summonsed to Exeter magistrates. The Chief Constable stated that she was an elderly lady somewhat confused after a collision (well, she was 56!). In the event, the case was dismissed but she had to pay 4s costs!

The John family were not the only visitors from London to Ethel in Crantock. In the late 1930's, sister Ursula met Benjamin Britten while he was on holiday in Crantock. Britten spent at least two summer holidays in Crantock and, when he returned from New York in 1942 with Peter Pears, he stayed with Ursula in her London residence in Chelsea. In appreciation, Britten dedicated his "A Ceremony of Carols" to her. Their relationship continued and it was Ursula who assembled and trained the choir to perform the premier of Britten's choral work, "St Nicolas" in 1948.

Ethel survived until 1960 when she died in St Austell at 81 (so clearly she came to live permanently in Cornwall) and sister Ursula lived in London until 1968 when she died aged 82.

We will never know how much the Nettleships, the Johns and the Praters interacted but they were all in the London "circuit" that existed around the 1910's/1930's Bohemian clique and they were all in Crantock at around the same time.

There was also another artistic "type" in the village, Charles Macpherson, a retired Professor from the Royal Academy of Music who lived at Kareena and died there in March 1941.

So, Crantock in the 1920s and '30s was a bit like today. An interesting collection of people; artists, intellectuals, retired professionals and "locals". Indiscriminate house building, some dull and some "cutting" edge, such as Boskenna and Sandy Close. People were complaining about too many ugly buildings. There were many "up-country" people with second homes in the village. Holiday lets were becoming common and caravan sites were spreading around the Beacon and Quarry Field.

Finally, just a few more threads for you!

1920. The steamer "Sandfly" foundered off the Kelseys
Aug 1924 there was an impressive wedding of Doreen Walker (a surgeon) from Bath and John Nixon (also a surgeon) from Bristol the service was conducted by the brother of the bridegroom & cousin of the bride who came down from Westminster Abbey where he was Precentor to the Dean. Does anybody know why this wedding was in Crantock?
1930, the Rev Lawrence Ormerod who was a temporary curate for the parish was charged with assaulting a young girl from Zelah. Despite his behaviour, he took a young girl in his pony trap and visited her at her home, seeming

to be entirely inappropriate today, he was cleared of any misdemeanour.

1931 the Dartmoor Otter hounds had a miserable day on the Gannel and found nothing.

1932 Sarah Harris was caught re-handed by Constable Snell (who had concealed himself in a hedge) stealing hens' eggs from Philip Tonkin at Trevella. She was bound over to keep the peace for 12 months)

1935 a sea monster was sighted at Fernpit by the ferryman Mr Northey (must have been a slow summer?)

And finally, finally does anybody know why the Lincoln golf club awarded The Crantock Cup in 1929 (and again in 1951) for a lady's competition?

CHAPTER 9

WRECK & RESCUE

The first newspaper report of an incident at Crantock dates from November, 1807, when a brig called the *Ann* was driven ashore with the loss of three lives from the crew of five. At least two other ships also suffered serious damage although one, the naval tender *Bolina*, under Lieutenant Claribut, succeeded in avoiding the shore but lost one mariner over-board. The *Ann*, under Captain Phillips, who was sadly drowned, was en route from London to Bristol with a cargo of hemp, tallow and iron. A company of dragoon guards was dispatched from Truro to both help in the rescue attempts and to protect the cargo from potential looting. Clearly they were effective as all of the cargo was saved and the ship was so lightly damaged that she was recovered in the next week.

At the beginning of the nineteenth century, wrecking and looting still occurred, and the *James* (it may have been *Jane*), a smack belonging to Crouch & Sons, Falmouth, carrying flour and oats was attacked by a crowd of people from St Agnes when it came ashore on Perran sands in late December 1838. All of the crew were drowned as the ship was overwhelmed by the surf. Much of the cargo was washed ashore and plundered by the locals, who also stole the masts, rigging and sails. In fact, the ship was almost saved but, as it was being warped alongside the quay at St Agnes, the ropes parted and the *James* was wrecked on the rocks. The local people immediately looted the wreckage and took away all the remaining cargo despite the presence of the Preventative men. The Royal Cornwall Gazette carried an impassioned article condemning this *"unchristian and inhuman offence"* and that there were still *"persons in Cornwall, who have not been thoroughly reclaimed from the barbarism of past times, by the religious and moral instruction so diffuse amongst us, and can only be corrected by shame and punishment"*. In their defence, it must be remembered that Cornwall was reliant on locally produced food such as potatoes and grain and it was not uncommon for these crops to fail. Just eight years after this event, Cornwall, like Ireland, suffered from potato blight that decimated the harvest and left many working-class people desperate for food.

In January 1839, North West England, around Liverpool, suffered what was described as a hurricane, with extensive damage to buildings and numerous ships, including several American packet ships wrecked. It was one of the worst storms of the nineteenth century. In this same month, Richard Stephens from the Manor House, West Pentire, found the name plate from a foreign ship, the *Alemene*, washed-up on Crantock beach and other wreckage was found on Newquay beaches from the *Anthony*, of Scarborough. In fact, the weather during the first three weeks of 1839 was so stormy that all of the ports on the exposed North Cornish were closed to shipping.

The impact of the storms led to a number of technical innovations. First, in Liverpool, funds were raised to purchase a steam-powered life-boat as a local steam tug had been very successful in saving lives from numerous wrecks. In Cornwall, Henry Trengrouse from Hayle, had developed a rocket system that could be used to fire lines from either a ship or the shore across to a vessel in distress. The system was adopted by the Royal Navy as early as 1818 and was carried on board many ships as a means of firing a line from ship to shore. The Trengrouse system was further developed during the 1820s by John Dennett. These rockets had a metal body with about 9lbs of solid fuel and weighed over 20lbs. They had a range of about 250yds. In the 1860s an improved two stage rocket system was developed and patented by Colonel Edward Boxer of the Royal Artillery. This system continued in service with the coast guards for many years

Today, it is hard to appreciate how many shipwrecks, either total or recoverable, took place around the Cornish coast during the nineteenth century. In this period, Cornwall relied on shipping to supply coal to the booming mining industry and to transport metal ores to the smelting works in South Wales. In addition, Cornwall was the first land-fall for many ships trading, not just with England but also the wider North European nations. Shipping reports in local newspapers bear testament to the hundreds of arrivals and departures from numerous ports, both large and small, such as Falmouth and Padstow. Newspapers also list several hundreds of shipwrecked sailors being accommodated in seamen's missions at these times.

In May, 1842, the smack *"Lady Willoughby"*, carrying a cargo of oats from Youghal, county Cork, was driven ashore at Crantock. The cargo was lost but the ship was saved and eventually sailed around to Newquay where she docked in August. This was quite a typical scenario, ships would be driven ashore but they would be salvaged and returned to service. In fact, Lady Willoughby, under a new master, survived until at least 1845 when she finally disappeared from Lloyd's Register.

In May 1845 the 65 ton schooner *St Agnes*, built in Bideford and based in St Ives, was hit by a large wave off Perran beach. The wave badly damaged her rudder so that she became unmanageable. The three crew, under Captain Richards, managed to launch a boat and row to Carter's Rocks off Holywell. The schooner, with her cargo of coal, eventually struck the Chick and was smashed to pieces. The four survivors landed on Carter's Rocks but had to wait over 24 hours before they were rescued. The sea was so rough that it was not possible to reach them from Newquay and so a Mr Hoblyn from Perran sent a man with a horse and cart to St Ives to raise the alarm. The *Thomas* sailed from St Ives and finally managed to rescue the four men on the following day. Carter's rocks are also called Gull rocks. According to a letter from Richard Newton to the Royal Cornwall Gazette in 1858, the rocks were named after the Carter family (forbears of the Hoblyn family who lived at Trevornick) that once owned the mainland. More recent marketing has it that they are named after the smuggling Carter brothers (who were from the Penzance area), the most infamous of which, John Carter, is recalled in the song the *"King of Prussia"*. Incidentally, Mr Newton's letter suggested blasting Penhale headland to create a large natural harbour sheltered behind the rocks to create a refuge for shipping between St Ives and Padstow.

Two years later, in December 1847, the *Marchioness of Abercorn*, the largest ship ever to come ashore at Crantock was beached with the loss of three lives but all the cargo and over twenty passengers and crew were saved. This rescue is described in detail elsewhere in this booklet.

In the previous year, July 1846, the East Wheal Rose lead mine was flooded when the river Gannel overflowed following a violent thunderstorm over Newlyn Downs. This resulted in very significant changes to the river with huge quantities of silt being deposited down-stream. The river trade never recovered from this inundation and soon all of the lead ore from Newlyn and the iron ore from Perran was being exported from the developing harbour at Newquay with is rail and tram-way link to Par. However, the river still had significant flood and ebb-tides, probably far more than today, and in June 1848 a young man was driving a horse and cart loaded with sand back from Crantock along the Gannel. He had delivered a load of lead ore from East Wheal Rose mine, presumably to the small smelting works opposite Fernpit. Sadly, the horse fell into a whirlpool some 16 feet deep and, whilst the young driver was saved, the horse drowned. To compound the tragedy, not an hour after the body of the horse had been recovered, a second, two-horse wagon being driven by a fifteen year old boy, Joseph Heffernon, fell into the same pit. The boy had been following the tracks of the previous cart, thinking this was a safe passage. Both horses and driver were drowned.

February, 1853, witnessed the schooner *Comet* on voyage from Cardiff to Hayle wreck at Crantock but all the crew were rescued by the coastguards using their Dennett's rocket apparatus.

The dangers of the river Gannel were again demonstrated in the summer of 1857 when a young man was caught in a whirlpool beneath East Pentire and drowned when he lost his footing. The following year, 1858, saw the arrival into the Gannel of the first metal steam ship, the *Killarney* of 500 tons collecting iron ore from the Perran mines. This was probably the largest vessel to come into the Gannel and it presaged the period over which sailing ships would be replaced by steam power. This change would clearly have a major impact on shipping. Steam ships were not subject to the vagaries of wind and tide in the same way that sailing ships were.

The following year, 1859 was very eventful, there were at least two, if not three, significant earthquakes along the Cornish coast, or, as the newspapers described them "Extraordinary Agitations"! The 'quakes of June and early October were clearly accompanied by minor tsunamis that left fish stranded in the Fal, schooners beached at Par and a wave, three-feet high, sweeping along the Truro river from Malpas. There were also at least three major storms, in April, October and November with significant loss of shipping.

In late October, winds of around 100mph battered the west coast, from Cornwall to Scotland. The storm raged with force 12 winds for over 2 days and, on the second day, the 26th of October, the 2,700 ton steam clipper the *Royal Charter*, en route from Melbourne to Liverpool was driven ashore and wrecked on Anglesea. At least 450 people died, and only 39 (all men) survived. The passengers included many gold miners returning home having made their fortunes. Not only were the miners carrying large quantities of gold but the ship was also carrying a cargo of gold. It was rumoured that many locals became extremely rich on the gold that they "liberated" from the wreck. Scuba divers continue to make the occasional find of gold fragments. Monty

Don's great-great- grandfather died in the wreck that gave its name to the storm; The Royal Charter storm.

During this period, there was a growing trade between Australia and UK that triggered significant competitions between steam clipper ships, such as the *Royal Charter*, and pure sailing ships. The Royal Charter was one of the first large ships to employ a clipper rig supplemented by steam driven screw propellers. In favourable conditions, sailing ships were far faster than steam powered propeller ships. The propellers were only used when the ship was becalmed, such as passing through the doldrums. The propellers could be raised clear of the water in order to reduce drag when these ships were sailing. When the *Royal Charter* began service on the UK to Australia route in 1856, she set a record by arriving in under 60 days. This was heralded as a major step-forward in long-distance travel but the owners of sailing ships were not to be so easily outdone! Only a year before the wreck, the *Royal Charter* had been beaten on the voyage from Melbourne to Liverpool by a schooner belonging to the famous Black Ball Line. The schooner also beat the sixty day mark and arrived in Liverpool eight days ahead of the steam clipper.

The North coast of Cornwall was very badly affected by Royal Charter storm. A major reason for this was that many vessels were trying to take advantage of big spring tides that meant that entry to several of the Cornish ports was made easier and they could carry more cargo with the additional draught (It would be another seventeen years before the Load Line (Plimsoll Line) would become compulsory on British shipping). Also, the weather was relatively calm, only twenty-four hours before the storm there were gentle South Easterly winds. Unfortunately, when the storm did strike the wind shifted very rapidly around to the North West which put all the Bristol channel fleet onto a lee shore.

Out of six ships that left Cardiff with cargoes of coal for St Ives, Hayle and Padstow. Only one ship, the *Liberty* under Capt Andrews made it. The Doom bar claimed the *Sultana Selina* with the loss of all seven crew. The *Pearl* was wrecked at St Agnes and the *Thistle* at the appropriately named Morte Bay, North Devon, although all crew were saved from these vessels. However, between St Agnes and Newquay, a further six ships were driven ashore.

The *Mary Ann* from Plymouth, bound for Ilfracombe, was beached at Perran on 25th with a crew of four; father, two sons and one sailor. Only the elder son George Ridge was saved after clinging to the rigging for eight hours. The *Caroline*, bound from Neath to Weymouth was also driven ashore at Perran but the crew of three were saved. The *Ann*, a Penzance boat, was wrecked in Newquay together with a French lugger *Anais* en route from Cardiff to Nantes. The crew of the *Ann* was rescued but there were difficulties with the French ship because the crew could not understand the instructions from the coastguard team who managed to fire a rope across the vessel using their Dennett's rockets. In the end, the head of the coastguards (William Tregidgo), *"with a courage that sent a thrill through every one who witnessed his noble daring, rushed into the surf up to his neck, and directed the crew"*. In this way, all six were brought ashore *"amidst the acclamation of the spectators"*. Tregidgo was awarded a medal by the French for this rescue.

There was no rest for the coastguard crew, no sooner had they rescued the French crew, when news reached them that two vessels were driven ashore on Crantock beach; a French schooner, the *Union* bound from Cardiff to Bordeaux, and another *Ann* on voyage to Milford from Plymouth. Mr Tregidgo, *"drenched to the skin"*, immediately went to Crantock and again managed to fire ropes across the *Union* after two attempts and four of the crew were recovered. A fifth crew-member had already been swept away but saved by a local fisherman who waded out through the surf. The crew of the *Ann* came ashore when the tide ebbed and left the vessel stranded. Three of the six ships were totally wrecked.

As a result of his actions, William Tregidgo was awarded a third Service Clasp by the National Life-boat Institution. It was not until the following year that the Institution was granted its Royal Charter. There was some criticism of the Duchy of Cornwall for failing to provide a life-boat on this stretch of the coast: *"and had the Duchy of Cornwall extended that help to our shores which might so naturally have been expected from it, one might have been here long ago"*.

William Tregidgo served in the coastguards all of his working life. He was born in Falmouth in 1813 and worked at various coastguard stations around the Cornish coast. Before his transfer to the Newquay station he had served as Chief Boatman at Stratton, Bude. He remained in Newquay for the rest of his life and later became secretary of the Newquay lifeboat committee on his retirement from the coastguards. In

1870 charges were brought against Tregidgo by the Receiver of Wrecks, Mr Bryant, for failure to provide assistance at the wreck of the *Suez* at Watergate beach. He was also charged with cowardice and failure to give evidence against some local watermen for obstructing Bryant during the inquiry following the *Suez* wrecking. An independent inquiry by the Lords Commissioners of the Admiralty dismissed all charges and Tregidgo was exonerated.

The case of the 354 ton, Austrian owned *Suez* raised considerable interest in Cornwall. She was a three-masted barque captained by Guiseppe Perovich, carrying a cargo of maize from the Black Sea. When she came ashore in January 1870, the Newquay lifeboat was launched and succeeded in taking the crew of ten, including the Captain, back to Newquay where they were met by Mr Michell from the Fort (chairman of the lifeboat society) and Mr Hicks, honorary agent for the Shipwrecked Mariners' Association. It all seemed to be a very successful rescue. However, the following day, the Captain and Mr Bryant, the Receiver of Wrecks agreed that the vessel could be salvaged. A steam tug, the *Gladiator* from Cardiff, was engaged and arrived on the Tuesday. Mr Bryant had made an agreement with the lifeboat committee that the lifeboat could be used to transfer a team of local men out to the *Suez* to assist in the salvage. However, when a crew was requested, Mr Matthews, a local boatman and member of the lifeboat crew, threatened to *"knock off Mr Bryant's head"* if the lifeboat was launched. Bryant offered £5 per man but Matthews stood before a growing crowd and said, *"Mind, any man entering that boat shall be beaten"*. It is clear that the Newquay men wanted to take control of the salvaging of the *Suez* and bring her into Newquay for financial reasons! This was despite the fact that both the insurers and the local officials thought the ship too big to attempt to bring it into the quay. In the end, the tug went to Padstow and gathered a boarding party who succeeded in taking the ship back to Padstow. Matthews was charged at St Columb petty sessions with unlawfully endeavouring to impede the saving of a certain ship and cargo. Tregidgo gave evidence that Matthews was a *"very good man in a lifeboat, always ready to save life, but he had acted very badly in this case"*. Matthews was found guilty and fined £20 and expenses. Two other men, Henry and William Clemens were also involved in the affair but charges against them were subsequently dropped.

The reason this case attracted so much attention was that it demonstrated that the old traditions associated with wrecking and demanding money for salvage still persisted. "Making an example" of the local boatmen who tried to prevent the officials from acting lawfully was seen as an important message to be made to other people in the coastal communities of Cornwall.

After fifteen years as the secretary to the Newquay lifeboat service, William Tregidgo died in December

1883. His wife died within a few hours of him and they were buried at a joint funeral during which all the shops were closed and ships in the harbour flew their flags at half-mast.

The Newquay lifeboat station had a chequered history during its early years. The first National Lifeboat Institute boat, the *Moses (or was it the Joshua?)*, arrived in September 1860 through a donation from a "benevolent lady" who also financed a sister boat at St Ives. The boat was not involved in many rescues and the *Suez* incident was probably the most notable. The boat was replaced in 1874 by the *Pendock Neale*, again financed primarily through a bequest, in this case from Miss Neale. The *Pendock Neale* was involved in many rescues including

several bizarre incidents. In the spring of 1874 she was called to a very large ship, the 1500 ton *Gottenburg*, off Penhale. The lifeboat rescued all 18 crew and they managed to secure the ship with her anchors. The following day, the captain engaged the Penzance based steamer, the *Queen of the Bay*, to tow the *Gottenburg* to Falmouth. However, and unbeknown to the captain, the small steamer *Victoria*, based in Hayle, reached the Gottenburg under cover of fog and took her in tow after slipping her anchors. Not unreasonably, the captain was not best pleased by this action and commandeered the Newquay lifeboat and crew to give chase. Somehow the lifeboat, under canvas alone, managed to overhaul the *Victoria* and the captain jumped on board and cut the tow rope! Luckily the *Queen of the Bay* had arrived by this time and was able to take the large ship in tow. The wind had increased so much that it was not possible for the lifeboat to make headway back to Newquay and so she too was towed around to Falmouth and returned by road after being rowed up to Truro. Although the rescue was a success, an article in a local paper expressed concern that only two of the lifeboat crew were regular members. It was subsequently reported that Newquay was struggling to man their lifeboat because so many men were being employed to build the Cornwall Mineral Railway line into the town. Further, many local seamen were migratory, spending part of the year fishing and part of the year working as crew on larger merchant ships. It was also stated that the coxswain of the lifeboat had been very ill, in fact he died.

This was not the last time that the Newquay lifeboat station came in for criticism. In August, 1880, the small Barnstaple built sailing smack, *Harriet*, carrying coal from Swansea to Hayle was seen to be in trouble off Fistral beach. She eventually ran onto the rocks on the point of East Pentire, probably Zarven, at around 9pm and was a total wreck. However, her crew of two, managed to launch their boat and row into the lee of Goose Rock. A large crowd had gathered to watch and the *Pendock Neale* was towed to the harbour to launch. However, the coxswain, Edwin Clemens, was unable to muster a crew willing to attempt the rescue. Because of the lack of a permanent crew, any lifeboat launch was dependent on volunteers, often drawn from the crew of visiting ships. It was not until 3am, the following morning, when the storm had abated and the seas dropped that enough volunteers came forward to attempt the rescue. Amazingly, the two men had managed to keep their small boat in the relatively safe waters in the lee of the Goose and they were eventually rescued and landed in Newquay harbour at 7am. The Cornishman newspaper carried a scathing account of the rescue: *"It was the old, old story, alas! There were plenty of salts who had weathered many a storm, but there was a difficulty to get them to volunteer on this occasion, and even the majority of the regular crew of the lifeboat were nowhere to be found. Many were the expressions of righteous indignation last night by the people who had crowded to the scene of this heartrending affair"*.

Sadly, the Newquay lifeboat was in the news again in January 1895, when it failed to go to sea in similar circumstances. This time it resulted in a full Board of Trade inquiry at which the coxswain, still Edwin Clemens, was accused of cowardice. The steam ship *Escurial* (she also carried a schooner rig) left Cardiff bound for Fiume in Austria (modern-day Rijeka, Croatia) with a cargo of coal. She developed a list soon after leaving Cardiff and then ran into rough weather as she came along the north coast of Devon and Cornwall. At 2am on the 25th, flares were fired to indicate that she was in serious distress. The Newquay lifeboat maroons were raised and the coxswain, again Edwin Clemens, mustered in preparedness to launch. However only three crew appeared and the coxswain deemed it too dangerous to attempt a launch because the *Escurial's* position was not clear and there was an extremely high-sea running. The subsequent inquiry suggested that the lifeboat could have launched from the harbour at high-tide, around 6am. However, the coxswain refused to attempt this as there was no certainty about the position of the ship. It was finally agreed to try to launch the lifeboat from the beach at 11am but two attempts failed as the surf was so big and the lifeboat broached on each occasion. Eye witnesses suggested that the attempts had been somewhat half-hearted.

At mid-day, the *Escurial* struck Gull rock at Portreath. By this time, the Hayle lifeboat had been carted eleven miles by road to the beach at Portreath. Several attempts were made to launch but without success. A number of crew from the *Escurial* managed to jump into the sea and were carried to the shore using their cork-filled life-jackets. However, many of the crew refused to leave the ship and clung to the rigging on the masts. Attempts were made, not only by the lifeboat, but also by the coastguards firing rocket lines, to reach the stranded seamen. However, all failed and a single large wave broke the masts and rigging and threw all the remaining crew into the sea. Eleven men were drowned and nine were saved. It was the biggest loss of life from any wreck in the Portreath area and naturally attracted huge publicity. Much of the publicity focused on the failure of the Newquay lifeboat to launch when it may have been possible to save lives.

The subsequent inquiries made clear that the *Escurial* was perfectly seaworthy and no blame could be attributed to either the owners or the captain, who had drowned. One of the crew claimed that lifesaving equipment was inadequate and in a poor state of repair but this was not accepted by the board of inquiry and the man was later charged in a criminal court for perjury. A separate inquiry was ordered into the actions of the Newquay lifeboat service that concluded that the committee was failing to manage the station adequately. It was recognised that too many of the committee were extremely elderly and the training of the lifeboat crew was poor. The coxswain was considered to have been in service too long and possibly to have lost his nerve. The end result was a complete overhaul of the whole committee and the appointment of a new chairman, secretary, coxswain and deputy coxswain.

Perhaps the last major shipwreck to occur at Crantock was a year before the *Escurial* when the 120 ton schooner *Expert* signalled distress as she was crossing Crantock bay in January 1894. The Newquay lifeboat was launched but could not make any headway once it rounded Towan head because of the gale force westerly wind and high seas. Rocket equipment was also dispatched but was too late. The ship struck the rocks off

East Pentire and the crew of four was thrown into the sea along with a large retriever dog. Sadly, all were killed. Two of the crew were natives of Appledore where the captain's two sons also lived. One of the crew, James Fox, was the third son of a former coxswain of the Appledore lifeboat to have been drowned as a result of ship-wreck. In a newspaper report of the time, the ship was *"dashed on the sharp jagged rocks which, in summer time are such a delight to visitors, but which during a storm are such a dread for mariners"*. This is an early reference to visitors and suggests the transition from Crantock and the Gannel being primarily associated with agriculture and shipping towards a holiday destination.

Crantock beach and the Gannel began to see more leisure activities from the time that it ceased to be a significant port as a result of silting and the growth of Newquay harbour. The number of shipwrecks reduced, not just because of its demise as a port but also with the transition from sail to steam and more robust and powerful ships. Unfortunately, the number of accidents involving swimmers and other water-users became more common. Perhaps the most distressing accident occurred in 1872 when a party of people who were visiting Silas Martyn at Tregunnel decided to take a small sailing boat on the river after taking tea. Silas was married to Harriet Johns, a sister of Jane Trindade. Silas and Harriet had seven children, William, Silas, Mary Jane, Edward Lawer, Julia Ann, Richard John and Silas Hiscott. From all accounts, there was a significant wind blowing but the party of five crossed the river to the Crantock side before turning and heading back. Unfortunately, on the way back, there was a sudden gust of wind and the boat capsized. Silas Hiscott Martyn (18) was badly hurt in the capsize and was heard to shout "Oh Ned we shall all be drowned". These were his final words as he was swept away from the upturned boat. The two men, Captain (probably a title associated with the mining industry) Edward Martyn (27) and Joel Rowe, from Trethellan, took hold of the two girls, Bessie Tremaine and Elizabeth Hawke, both from St Columb and tried to swim to the shore. Sadly, all of the party were dressed in heavy clothing that became waterlogged so that the two men were unable to keep their heads above water and they had to abandon the girls to save themselves.

The end result was that three of the party were drowned; Silas Hiscott Martyn, Bessie Tremaine and Elizabeth Hawke (who was the sister of Mr Hawke the draper in Newquay, that would eventually become Madam Hawke, that is today Costa Coffee). The inquest recorded accidental drowning. No blame was apportioned and the men were praised for their efforts to save the girls.

From this date onwards, reported drownings become increasingly common in the press. Many were attributed to the dangers of the river, that in some accounts had a course that ran across the beach. There are also more references to visitors in the village although the account of schoolchildren on a summer holiday contracting typhoid in August 1881, was probably not welcome news! It appears that Crantock was a favourite spot for people from Truro and other Cornish towns to have summer chalets. A newspaper advertisement in May 1886 listed an auction of West Pentire farm together with 3 dwellings that had served as summer residences for many years. The advertisement also noted that there were several desirable building sites within the farm boundary! Crantock was changing and would rapidly become a favourite village for the growing tourist industry, encouraged by the Great Western Railways and the extensive railway network. By the 1920's many chalets had been built and camping facilities were established at Quarry Field and the Beacon (Crantock Bay).

There are many accounts of people getting into difficulties while swimming at Crantock in the early twentieth century. One of the saddest is that of Sister Emilie and two young girls under her care during an outing in June 1908. Sister Emilie came from the Convent of the Epiphany in Truro. In 1908, a chapel was added to the original house by the architect Edmund Sedding who had been responsible for the renovation of Crantock church. The convent was sold in 1983 and is now the Alverton Hotel.

Sister Emilie brought around 20 girls to Crantock for a two week holiday at the Manor House, West Pentire. The girls were from the Rosewin Training School for

Servants that was attached to the convent. On Tuesday, 23 June, they all went down to the cove at West Pentire for an al fresco lunch, to be followed by a swim. It was around half ebb-tide and the party was sitting on the rocks in the cove waiting until the little beach was accessible. It appears that there was a very big ground sea running (reports suggested 15 ft waves in the bay) and a large wave swept a small group of girls off the rocks. Sister Emilie, despite being a non-swimmer, ran to their aid but was also washed off by a second wave and knocked unconscious. Of the girls swept into the sea, two were swept away but two managed to stay afloat while others scrambled to safety. A number of local people, who had seen what was happening, ran to the scene and dived into the sea. Mr Rowe and Captain Fenton managed to recover the two girls who were floating, Isabella Miriams and Dorothy Wood. However, despite their efforts they were unable to locate either Sister Emilie or the two girls who were swept away and whose bodies were seen floating out in the bay.

The two girls who drowned were Mary Jane Searle, 13, originally from Penzance and Annie Sophie Frost, 14, from Sussex. Mary had been sent to the school from the Penzance workhouse after her mother died. Their bodies were recovered nearly two weeks later off Newquay headland and they were buried by Rev Metford Parsons in Crantock on 9 July. Their metal grave marker is still in the churchyard on the right-hand side as you approach the church. Sister Emilie's body was not recovered until the 9 July when a fisherman found it off Port Isaac. It was said that her body was in perfect condition with no trace that it had been in the water for two weeks. She was still wearing her crucifix and she was buried in St Endellion churchyard on 10 July.

Following this terrible accident, the coroner advised Crantock Parish Council to install life-lines and lifebelts at the scene. Five years earlier, in 1903, Edith Greenstreet and her maid Kate Wilkes had been drowned at the same point and the coroner at their inquest had made a similar recommendation. It was noted at the inquest, by the Coroner (Mr E L Carlyon), that it was important that West Pentire should not be confused with Newquay as this would have an adverse impact on tourism because *"a safer beach could not be found in England than that at Newquay"*. He wanted to *"make it absolutely clear that West Pentire is a considerable distance from Newquay"*!

In the summer, the Rosewin Home had to cancel its fundraising fete, upon which it depended for funds, which led to an appeal for donations to support the work of the Sisters. Several of the rescuers were awarded medals by the Royal Humane Society. These included the rescued Isabella Miriams, the daughter of Augustus Mirams a London barrister. She was learning Japanese at the school before travelling to Japan as a missionary.

Crantock continued to feature in the press throughout the first half of the twentieth century for incidents involving drownings and dramatic rescues. Until the lifeguard service was properly established in the late 1950's and early 1960's, the beach averaged around one drowning every four or five years; it was not considered to be a safe beach. Fortunately, things have changed with the arrival of professional life-savers and, whilst the beach continues to challenge water users, the number of fatal accidents has declined markedly.

CHAPTER 10

Dr Edward Bouverie Pusey

At the west side of Crantock beach, just after the Piper's Hole cave, there is a ramp and set of steps cut into the rocks leading up to West Pentire. These are known as Pusey's steps and they are named after the Reverend Edward Bouverie Pusey who was responsible for creating the pathway to both ease the trip to the freshwater spring and to provide access to the beach for the inhabitants of the small hamlet of West Pentire. But, who was Edward Pusey and what is his connection to West Pentire?

Edward Bouverie Pusey was born in the Berkshire village of Pusey, not to be confused with Pewsey, on 22 August 1800. He was the second son of Philip Bouverie who adopted the name Pusey when he succeeded to the manor on the death of his father, Jacob des Bouverie, the 1st Earl of Folkestone. Edward had an older brother, Philip, and a sister, Charlotte. Philip, who was only one year older than Edward, was to become a leading figure in the world of agriculture and was a founding member of the Royal Agricultural Society. He was also a Member of Parliament for Berkshire, Fellow of the Royal Society and close friend of Sir Robert Peel. Disraeli described him as *"one of the most distinguished country gentlemen who ever sat in the House of Commons"*. He was actively involved in the Great Exhibition of 1851 but sadly died just five years later at the age of fifty-six. As with his more famous brother, he was very regularly reported in the West Country press because of his many publications, particularly relating to the breeding and rearing of sheep on water-meadows. He is credited with developing earthenware drainage systems for use in marshy fields.

Younger brother Edward was educated at Eton college before going to Christ Church college, Oxford. This was to begin a life-long association with Oxford university. He graduated with a first-class honours degree in 1822 and was elected to a fellowship at Oriel college in 1824. Between 1825 and 1827 he studied oriental languages and German theology at Göttingen where he published his first academic papers.

In 1828, the Prime Minister, the Duke of Wellington, appointed Pusey to the Regius Chair of Hebrew at Oxford. Pusey took holy orders in the same year and was appointed Canon of Christ Church. He also married Maria Catherine Barker to whom he had become engaged the previous year. His courtship of Maria had been difficult as her father was strongly opposed to their marriage. It was not until after her father died that Edward's proposal was accepted. Edward and Maria only had eleven years together before she died from tuberculosis in 1839. They had four children, all of which suffered from serious health issues. Three daughters died young and only their son Phillip survived to adulthood. He followed his father into the English church but suffered from tuberculosis throughout his life and predeceased his father. In fact, Edward was also plagued with ill-health throughout his life and often retreated to the coast to "take the sea air".

During the next few years, Pusey published a number of papers on theology that were considered by some of the established Anglican church to be radical. His experiences in Germany led him to propose a return to more catholic interpretations of Anglicanism – Anglo-Catholicism, that we would term "high church". It was at this time that he became a leading member of the "Oxford Movement", sometimes called the Tractarians, that included John Keble and John Henry Newman, who was also a Fellow of Oriel college. Newman would eventually turn away from the Anglican church and convert to the Catholic church in October 1845. Newman became a leading member of the Roman Catholic church and would eventually be canonised as a saint in 2019.

After Pusey's promotion to the Chair, the Oxford Movement published a number of Tracts, each dealing with a specific area of Anglican beliefs. Pusey contributed a number of notable papers dealing with subjects such as fasting and baptism. He became very influential in the Oxford Movement, it was even termed Puseyism by some, and was instrumental in creating the theological bases for proposed changes to conventional Anglicanism. Although he was not recognised as a great orator, his sermons were widely published and served as a source of inspiration and detail for the more eloquent communicators of the Movement. In 1843, Pusey preached a sermon, *The Holy Eucharist a Comfort to the Penitent*, that caused a major controversy with the Anglican establishment and the Vice Chancellor of Oxford suspended him from preaching for the next two years. The immediate effect was that over eighteen thousand copies of the sermon were sold and Pusey gained a wide-spread following across the Anglican community. Clearly, religion was a far more central issue for British society during the nineteenth century compared with today. Over the next twenty years, there are very many newspaper reports detailing both Pusey's publications and the, sometimes vitriolic responses that they drew from the more traditional Anglicans. A contemporary description of Pusey, immediately following his controversial sermon in 1843, sums up the antipathy that he had generated: *"I turned my eyes towards the door, and saw one or two official persons opening a way of approach down the aisle by which I was sitting. Immediately following them came Dr Pusey, wearing a gown or robe of some other name, half black and half red. He appeared to be of short stature, five feet four or five inches high, and somewhere between fifty and sixty years of age (he was 43). Perhaps he is not so old. His thin features, seen through a shrivelled skin, bare and brown, contrasted with the full red rosy faces of most of the other doctors of divinity present. I do not recollect to have ever seen a head in the lower part of its fabric so unsubstantial, with a brow so dome-like as Doctor Pusey's. He has no remarkable development of the reflective faculties as seen phrenologically; but he is strong in the higher regions of the brain – in veneration, hope, wonder, ideality, and so on."*

The next two years proved extremely testing for Pusey. He was deeply upset by his suspension and actively fought the decision. He seems to have divided his time between the family home at Pusey and trips to see his supporters and old colleagues. During this time his son, Philip, was sent to a school in Brighton and his two surviving daughters, Lucy and Mary, lived with a guardian in Clifton. In April 1844 his oldest daughter, Lucy, died. This was another major blow for Pusey as, although only a teenager, she had already committed her life to the Church. It was her hope to establish some form of Anglican Sisterhood to promote good works amongst the poorer communities. Soon after Lucy died, Pusey preached his first sermon since being suspended at Oxford. This was at Ilfracombe where he spent most of the summers of both 1844 and 1845. In order to preach at an Anglican church while suspended from Oxford, he had to obtain permission from the Bishop of Exeter. He travelled to Ilfracombe with his two surviving children on a steamer from Clifton.

The next major blow was when his very close friend and mentor, Newman, converted to Roman Catholicism in October 1845. This made Pusey an even more important figure within the Oxford Movement. However, 1845 also saw the completion of the building of a St Saviour's church in Leeds that he had funded. His connection with Leeds was through another close friend from his days as an undergraduate at Oxford, Walter Hook. Pusey was always very generous in his support for charitable works and providing financial support to good causes. He and his wife had previously sold their horses and carriage, together with all her jewellery, to provide funds for the Bishop of London's initiatives amongst the poor in the East End. Indeed, he often visited the East End in London and, in March 1845, he initiated the first Anglican Sisterhood, the Sisters of Mercy, under Miss Langstone as the Superior, near St Pancras; his daughter's vision had been achieved. 1845 also saw Pusey's Oxford suspension lifted but he continued to deliver questioning sermons and publish controversial academic papers throughout the rest of his life.

In 1848 the Bishop of Exeter advertised for help with the poor in Devonport, particularly for new churches and education. Miss Lydia Sellon responded to the request, encouraged by her father, Richard Baker Smith, who would have had first-hand experience of the social conditions in the area around the naval dockyard as he had service as a Royal Naval Commander. He had remarried after Lydia's mother died and went on to have eleven more children at his home in Devon. He also changed his name to Sellon after receiving a significant inheritance from his maternal aunt.

Lydia sought support from Pusey (she was twenty one years younger than him), who she already knew from his work with the London Sisterhood. He put her in contact with the Devonport clergy and over the next few years Lydia succeeded in creating an industrial school for girls, an orphanage for sailors' children, a school for the starving and a night school for teenage boys. Clearly, Lydia was a very determined and effective organiser. Contemporary reports suggest that she was extremely autocratic! In 1849, together with the women that worked with her, she formed the Devonport Sisters of Mercy (or the Sisterhood of the Holy Trinity), probably the second Anglican Sisterhood. In the same year she coordinated efforts to contain and treat a major outbreak of cholera in Devonport, an experience that served her well in the subsequent training of the sisterhood in nursing methods. Unfortunately, Miss Sellon (all references refer to her as Miss Sellon rather than Lydia) also caught cholera and would spend the rest of her life as a semi-invalid. Her Sisterhood merged with the original London based Sisterhood in 1849 and Miss Sellon took over leadership of the combination, referring to herself as the Abbess.

In 1851, Miss Sellon "hit the headlines" after she wrote to the Lord Chief Justice of England, Lord Campbell asking (begging) him to withdraw his name from the list of those people supporting her Devonport Sisterhood. Her request had been prompted by some statements made by Lord Campbell during a court case that she interpreted as being contrary to her views of the Anglican Church. A vast amount of correspondence resulted from this action and it unleashed many pent-up feelings from within the Church. Over the next two years, the newspapers were filled with really vicious attacks against the Sisterhood and Pusey. Eminent people withdrew support for the Devonport Sisterhood. Women who had withdrawn from the Sisterhood provided much salacious gossip about what went on inside and how everything was based on Roman Catholic principles. In short, these were not Anglican orders but Roman Catholic nunneries deliberately subverting Anglicanism to invade the Church of England. By association, therefore, the teachings of Pusey were not Anglican but Roman Catholic. Oxford and other universities were dismissed for *"producing large numbers of perverts to Romanism"* and the Sisterhoods would be *"handed over, bound hand and foot, to the abominations of Popery"*. It is difficult to understand the level of vitriol unleashed against Pusey and Miss Sellon over these two years. It appears that Miss Sellon was driven out of Plymouth and re-opened in Bristol in 1851. It is surprising that the Sisterhoods survived and even prospered in future years.

In 1858, Pusey was noted in the newspapers to be on holiday at Alverton house in Penzance with some members of the Sisters of Mercy. In the same year, Punch published a poem:

Pusey – Pusey – Gander,
Wither would he wander,
Up-stairs, down-stairs,
And to my Lady's Chamber.
But Bull and Punch declare they wouldn't
Stand such priestly airs-
So took him by his shoulders,
And kicked him down-stairs.

There is an intriguing footnote about this period because a number of newspapers carried reports in December 1858 that Miss Sellon and Dr Pusey had married. This report was immediately rebutted by one of her brothers, John, in January of the following year. There is also a report in the Royal Cornwall Gazette in 1871 stating that Dr Pusey, Miss Sellon and party were spending a holiday at the Ponsmere Hotel in Perranporth. Make of that what you will! In the end, Miss Sellon pre-deceased him in 1876 after fifteen years as a wheel-chair bound invalid.

With the amalgamation of the two Sisterhoods, Miss Sellon set-about building a permanent base in parkland near Ascot. The Ascot priory was completed in 1860 and the combined Sisterhood moved there as a permanent home. The last member of the Sisterhood died in 2004. The Ascot Priory continues to this day as a centre for retreat and religious renewal. It is understood that Dr Pusey funded the construction of the priory set in forty acres of grounds, although others suggest that Miss

Sellon's family paid all the bills! In 1854 the Priory provided fourteen nuns to work with Florence Nightingale in the Crimea.

Pusey died in his small room at the Ascot Priory in September 1882 and was buried in the cathedral in Oxford where he had been canon for over fifty years. His funeral was a very grand affair and Prime Minister Gladstone was one of his pall bearers. After his death, his colleagues raised £50,000, bought a building in Oxford to house his library of books and provide an endowment to employ two librarians. The Pusey Library endures to this day.

So, what is the connection between this very celebrated theologian and West Pentire? There is reference to his visits in "Old Newquay", a booklet written by Sarah Teague Husband. Sarah Teague was born in 1850 and wrote her book in the 1920s. It contains very many interesting titbits of information about Newquay, often based on recollections of her parents who were born in the early quarter of the nineteenth century. Partly because the text is based on recollections, in some cases at third-hand, there are several inaccuracies, particularly around dates and detail. However, the booklet does provide many useful leads that stimulate more rigorous research through more reliable references, such as old newspapers.

According to Teague Husband, Pusey came to the area between 1853 and 1871, often staying for several months. It was observed that he stayed in Porth, West Pentire and Trenance. As noted, he was also reported by the local press to be visiting Perranporth in 1871. During his visits he became involved in several projects including improving steps at Porth, making it safer to walk between the island and the mainland. He is also credited with having been instrumental in improving the steps at West Pentire to enable easier access to freshwater and down to the beach, hence Pusey's steps. In 1863 Pusey put on an illuminated display at his lodgings in Prospect House, to celebrate the marriage of the Prince of Wales (later King Edward VII). The book also recounts a story about the local doctor, Dr Boyle, gathering snowdrops that he put under his silk top-hat to keep fresh. When the doctor met Pusey as he crossed the tramway at the bottom of Marky's Hill (Marcus Hill), he raised his hat and all the flowers cascaded to the ground. Pusey clearly found it amusing as the two highly qualified men scrabbled about between the railway lines to collect the snowdrops. Of course, everybody knows that Marky's hill got its name from Mark Cardell (aged 53) who, in a "fit of madness", in October 1853, cut his throat and ran all the way down the hill, across the Killacourt before leaping over the cliff to his death. Another gem from Teague Husband's book that does tie up with the registered death records!

What remains unclear is why Pusey spent so much time in this region as he does not appear to have any particular association with Cornwall, let alone the Newquay area. In his biography, written in 1894 by Henry Parry Liddon, there is only one reference to Cornwall. In 1858, one of Pusey's closest friends and supporters of the Oxford Movement, Charles Marriott, died but Pusey was unable to attend his funeral because he was in Cornwall and "too remote to travel".

The local folklore about Pusey suggests that he actually lived at the Manor House, West Pentire, when he was suspended from Oxford and that he continued to holiday there for many years. He is reputed to have taken a liking to a specific chair that became "Pusey's chair". In subsequent years, the church bought the chair where it now resides. It is thought to have been a "Bishop's chair" and that the owner of the guest-house, Mr Prater, had "come by it", possibly through his position as a church warden.

In fact, apart from the naming of the steps, there is little evidence to support any of these stories. His biography, that is extremely detailed and includes vast amounts of his correspondence, makes no mention of Crantock and only one reference to Cornwall. Enquiries to the Pusey library in Oxford similarly drew no reference to Cornwall, indeed, it was news to the librarians that he had ever come to Cornwall! His story typifies much local history where oral accounts have been handed down through generations and are often extremely difficult to verify. Like Jane Trinidade, there is obviously a firm base for the story but virtually no solid evidence that can be referenced. Perhaps Pusey only came to Crantock once but, because he was nationally famous, a tale became woven around him by locals that has become embedded in village folklore. That is what makes researching these tales so intriguing!